SEVEN FIRES

# SEVEN FIRES

## Grilling the Argentine Way

### Francis Mallmann

WITH PETER KAMINSKY

ARTISAN | NEW YORK

Published by Artisan
A division of Workman Publishing Company, Inc.
225 Varick Street
New York, NY 10014-4381
www.artisanbooks.com

Published simultaneously in Canada by
Thomas Allen & Son, Limited

Library of Congress Cataloging-in-Publication Data
Mallmann, Francis.
  Seven fires : grilling the Argentine way /
Francis Mallmann, with Peter Kaminsky.
      p.  cm.
   Includes index.
   ISBN 978-1-57965-354-5
   1. Cookery, Argentine. 2. Barbecue cookery. 3. Outdoor
cookery. I. Kaminsky, Peter. II. Title.
   TX716.A7M27  2009
   641.5982—dc22
                                        2008037367

Design by Jan Derevjanik
Principal photography by Santiago Soto Monllor
Recipe development by Donna Gelb and Lucía Soria

Printed in China

10 9 8 7 6

To Patagonia—the land of my childhood, the land that inspired my life.

Fire has its own language, spoken in
    the realm of heat, hunger, and desire.
It speaks of alchemy, mystery, and,
    above all, possibility.
It is a slumbering voice inside me
The ever-present beast within my soul
It is beyond words, beyond memory,
It comes from a time long before I can recall.

# Contents

# A Son of the Andes

The idea for this book grew out of a television series that Francis Mallmann made a few years ago, *Fires of the South*. He went on location in the wilds of wintry Patagonia to present the many varieties of wood-fire cookery. As you'll see, it is simple cooking, but at the same time truly inspired. You'll never taste a more succulent steak or a heartier winter stew. You'll discover that every fire has its own life and that from first spark to leaping flame

to smoldering ember, all the alchemy of combustion can be used to make great food. You may, as I have, come to rethink whatever opinion you had of barbecuing and grilling. In Francis's hands, the grill produces world-class gastronomy (a word that makes him cringe but which seems quite apt to me).

Francis is South America's most famous chef, a distinction helped in part by his movie-star looks and long-running career as the reigning star of food TV in the Spanish-speaking world. He's also a man of immense, highly personal style, but it is his skill and inspiration as a chef that remain the basis of his success and his fame.

Raised in the mountain town of Bariloche, the son of the nation's preeminent nuclear physicist, Francis was too high-spirited for his strict English-language boarding school. He spent the better part of his early adolescence on the nearby ski slopes and then took off for California, where he worked as a carpenter and street musician.

When he returned to Argentina two years later at the age of nineteen, he opened a restaurant in Bariloche. His innate kitchen talent and his suave front-of-the-house manner soon earned him a loyal following and his career took off. Within a few years, he had the opportunity to open a small restaurant in a tiny village about thirty miles up the coast from the jet-set resort of Punta

del Este, Uruguay. Fashionable Argentines spend weekends and summers here, just as New Yorkers flock to the Hamptons.

With the money he made during the holiday season in Uruguay, Francis could afford to close down when the vacationers left and intern in some of the most illustrious kitchens in France. Notable among them were those of Roger Vergé and Alain Senderens, which had six Michelin stars between them.

With that experience as his calling card and his subsequent success as a chef on Argentine television, Francis was soon the toast of Buenos Aires, but by the time he was forty, he was, in his words, "tired of making French food for wealthy Argentines." He wanted something else, something more fundamental and yet refined. The result was an evolving cuisine that he called Nuevo Andean, based on the wood-fire and cast-iron cooking practiced by generations of gauchos and Native Americans.

This is not to say that Francis jettisoned all the techniques of classic French cuisine that he had learned. Like any good French chef, he is a master of the art of intensifying, deepening, and developing all the flavors and textures of his ingredients. But rather than rely on complex sauces and architectural presentations, he keeps it simple. His list of ingredients for any recipe is usually short, the number of steps are few and simple. What makes his recipes so compelling is his mastery of wood fire.

A corollary of his return to his Andean roots was a nearly complete abandonment of the slow-cooked stocks and sauces canonized by Carême and Escoffier. In fact, in the dozen years I have known Francis, I don't believe I've ever seen a stockpot in his kitchen (although he has told me that he uses them occasionally). In place of classic sauces, he often dresses his food with olive oil and herb mixtures, adding vinegar or lemon juice for brightness.

Although simple cooking and gaucho rusticity were at the heart of his evolving style from the beginning, he set his table with white damask place mats and napkins from the artisanal looms of Le Jacquard Français in Paris and faience from Astard du Villete in Provence. His steak knives were handcrafted with wide shafts, long sharp points, and handles made of *huayacan,* a prized hardwood that grows on the slopes of Mount Tupungato, in the wine country of Mendoza.

It is now a dozen years ago since my friend Dana Cowin, the editor of *Food & Wine* magazine, asked if I would be interested in writing the text to accompany photographs taken at Francis's Patagonian lake house. She thought my fluency in Spanish would make the interview go more smoothly. But she needn't have concerned herself about that; Francis's accent was more British than Argentine and his English was thoroughly modern American. More Bob Dylan than Dylan Thomas.

Thus began a friendship between my family and his. There have been late-night dinners at his restaurant in La Boca—the Buenos Aires neighborhood where the tango was born—car treks the length of Patagonia, Christmases in Brooklyn, and Easters in Uruguay.

By this time, we are two members of a large family. This book, of Francis's recipes, is our invitation to you to join the family. Whether you cook these recipes over a campfire, on your backyard grill, or in your home kitchen, may you be—as we are—inspired by fire.

**—PETER KAMINSKY**

Francis Mallmann and Peter Kaminsky in Garzon, Uruguay.

# Baptized by Fire

My childhood home stood on a cliff overlooking Lago Moreno in Patagonia, where the snowcapped peaks of the Andes tower over everything. It was a simple but beautiful log house built by an English family in the 1920s and bought for my father by "Papapa," my grandfather Arturo. In that house, fire was a constant part of growing up for my two brothers and me, and the memories of that home continue to define me.

When I close my eyes and think back to those times, I can hear the breakfast conversation of my parents announcing the arrival of a truckload of firewood. The truck would dump the wood in the parking lot. We would all load up the wheelbarrows; my brothers and I would help in sorting and stacking the logs in the woodshed. When the work was done and the shed was packed to the roof with air-cured logs, I felt proud to be part of such a wealthy household.

Next came the ax work. My father, who was a physicist, saw it as an opportunity to get some exercise, while my brothers and I jumped at the chance to do "men's work." Every morning we would split some kindling to start the three fires that warmed us, heated our water, and fed our huge kitchen stove. This fire-belching behemoth was managed by Elsa, a cheerful Chilean cook who would go about her tasks pretending that she didn't notice me trying to steal a peek at her ample bosom.

I spent my early years as a culinary student and chef in some of the most famous kitchens of Europe, where I learned a lot about style as well as about food. Alain Senderens, the godfather of nouvelle cuisine, was one of my early masters. I was so impressed by his custom selection of Davidoff Havana cigars, each one, like vintage wine, named for a great château of Bordeaux.

The Provençal kitchen of Roger Vergé, where such soon-to-be-renowned chefs as David Bouley and Daniel Boulud also apprenticed, was no less inventive than Senderens's but here I learned that even a bustling kitchen can have a Zen calmness at its center. Vergé's food was light, bright in taste, as sunny as Provence itself. Then there was Raymond Oliver, perhaps the last great master of classic French cuisine. He wrote the monumental *La Cuisine* in his small office in the Palais Royale upstairs from his restaurant, the venerable Grand Véfour. One day, he called me into his office. He was holding the letter I'd sent him months before about my apprenticeship. The stationery bore my new logo—a copper pot—and beneath it was printed the motto "La nouvelle cuisine."

He looked at me for a long time. Then, with affection, he said, "My little South American, what value is this idiotic 'nouvelle cuisine' if you do not know the heritage of culinary tradition?" He smiled, gave me a signed copy of his book, and sent me back to the basement and eight cases of artichokes waiting to be trimmed.

Thus began the cure for my pretentiousness, culinary and otherwise. It ended years later when my cooking

**OPPOSITE:** In the farthest reaches of the Andes, in the depths of the Valdivian alpine rain forest, I light a fire when I arrive and never let it go out until the moment I leave.

returned to its "mother tongue": fire. The catalyst was a successful and, in retrospect, defiant meal that I served to some of the leading gourmets of Europe in 1995. The International Academy of Gastronomy—the most prestigious culinary organization in the world—had invited me to prepare a meal for them. I was in great company—such European superstars as Alain Ducasse, Ferran Adrià, and Frédy Girardet had received the same invitation, and I would be the first New World chef. The request was for a menu with a South American theme. The rest was left up to me.

I think a guardian angel—a very Argentine angel—whispered in my ear at that point. She suggested an entire menu featuring potatoes, the great gift of South America to the world's larder. I sent German Martinegui, who was at that time a chef in my Buenos Aires restaurant, to Cuzco, Peru—the royal capital of the Incas, where the greatest potatoes are grown. He had a simple shopping list: a thousand pounds of potatoes. For those of you who think of potatoes simply as the plain-looking things one sees in the supermarket, you have not yet seen the potato in all of its Andean glory. German came back to Buenos Aires with golden potatoes, red ones, purple, yellow, orange, marbled—and in all sizes, from little balls to big lumpy ovals barely distinguishable from a clod of dirt.

My crew and I filled our luggage with our precious edible cargo and flew to Frankfurt, where the academy dinner was being held at the Schloss Hotel, a fairy-tale castle. Thankfully, the customs inspectors were not on the lookout for a band of South American potato smugglers.

The manager of the hotel—a very formal old-school fellow—greeted me and asked, "How would you like to decorate the table?"

"With potatoes," I answered.

With perfect manners, as if potatoes were as natural in a centerpiece as roses, he inquired, "And what would you like the potatoes on?"

"Nothing," I said. "Just by themselves."

"Just the cloth?" he said, as if to prompt me to remember that the potatoes should go on a tray or platter of some sort. Certainly I couldn't mean naked potatoes on the beautiful white cloth. Could I?

"No, just the potatoes, unwashed, with the dirt still clinging to them."

The manager withdrew. He had probably learned that when dealing with lunatic chefs, it is best to leave before any possible knife play.

German and I piled potatoes about ten inches high, running down the center of the whole length of the table, and then set about preparing the meal.

It's traditional at academy events that the chef doesn't speak to the guests. Instead, he is invited in after the meal, when one member delivers a critique of the food on behalf of his fellows. But I felt I needed to explain what awaited them: nine courses, all of them featuring potatoes.

After the lunch, I entered to receive my "grades." They were very high. They were intended as much for the Andean potatoes as for the chef.

The president of the Italian branch of the academy asked to speak. He was a vigorous man of about eighty, trim and elegant. "Before I left Rome," he began, "I was very unsure about this 'potato feast.' In fact, the thought of coming to Germany to eat many potatoes soaked in oil gave me nightmares of indigestion. But what I have eaten today, I truly believe, was food made by the angels."

His words, and that event, had a profound effect on me. I was forty years old and very successful doing an Argentine version of contemporary fine dining. I had been at it for twenty-seven years.

A feeling of resolve came over me. I was through with the fancy sauces and the elaborately arranged ingredients piled high on the plate like one of Marie Antoinette's coiffures. I wanted to create a cuisine based on my Andean heritage. For inspiration, I turned to the methods of the frontier, of the gauchos and, before them, of the Indians.

My cuisine became, for want of a better word, barbaric in its attempt to achieve the pinnacle of flavors through the use of fire, whether the massive heat of a bonfire, or the slow steady warmth of dying embers.

To put it most simply, I returned to an Argentine cuisine of wood fire and cast iron. From that day to this, there has always been a fire burning somewhere in my life: in my home, in the kitchens of my restaurants, on the patio, at beach cookouts, at lakeside campfires. I am drawn to fire and the aroma of things cooking over wood.

To be sure, there are times when it is not practical to cook over a wood fire—but as I have found over the years, a charcoal fire, a gas grill, or even a cast-iron pan on the stove of a home kitchen can serve to create the texture and wonderful slightly burnt taste of open-fire cookery. Throughout this book, you will find instructions for cooking outdoors, but because I recognize that not all of you will always have access to open fire, you will also find instructions for how to achieve many of the same effects indoors. As long as you apply the same amount of heat to your food, then, regardless of the method or medium used—wood, charcoal, gas grill, cast iron—cooking will be successful. Of course, I always prefer a hardwood fire.

In this book, I share my versions of the recipes of a lifetime inspired by campfires and cattle drives, harvest festivals and fishing camps, street fairs and family Sundays. There are seven different fires that form the backbone of my cuisine. North Americans may recognize in them a kinship to barbecuing and charcoal grilling and will, I hope, find new possibilities in them. I've served these dishes to popes and presidents, prime ministers and kings, and, with equal success, to neighborhood kids in Buenos Aires and shepherds in the mountains of Patagonia.

May they kindle the same fire in your belly that they do in my soul.

## The Taste of Burnt

I adore dissonance in food—two tastes fighting each other. It wakes up your palate and surprises you. As you'll see in many of the recipes in this book, charring or even burning adds an extra dimension to breads, vegetables, and fruit. The right amount of burning or charring can be delicious and seductive: a burnt tomato, for example, has a dark crust bordering on bitter, while the inside is soft and gentle in texture and taste.

I believe that many chefs and cookbooks make entirely too much of harmony. Frankly, it can be boring. If you sleep in a very comfortable bed but sometimes take a siesta on the warm ground in the shade of a tree, you know that the experience of the one highlights the virtues of the other. In the same way, disharmony in cuisine calls attention to the basic nature of the ingredients. I'm not talking about some of the silly combinations attempted by novelty-seeking chefs—there's a difference between dissonance and a hopeless mismatch. What appeals to me is the element of danger and excitement in creating a burnt taste. Take the burning too far, and it destroys the dish. Stay just this side of the line, and it is lovely.

# My Argentina

Argentina is an enormous land, the eighth largest country on earth, stretching from the tropics in the far north to the solitary emptiness of Patagonia and Tierra del Fuego in the far south. It covers a little bit more area than the entire east *and* west coasts of the United States, with Texas thrown in for good measure. It has virtually every kind of climate, from arctic to tropical, and its geography ranges from rain forest to desert to alpine glaciers. Our

seasons are the reverse of North America's: August is normally our coldest month and February the hottest. Also reversed is the geography: the north is warm all through the year and the south is the last stop before chilly Antarctica.

The original Argentines were the Incas in the northwest, the descendants of the same people who built the great Peruvian empire, and, in the south, the exotic-sounding Onas, Yamanas, Tehuelches, and Mapuches, all of whom, preserve many of their old ways. These names are as familiar to Argentines as the Apaches, Cherokees, and Navajos are to North Americans.

Argentina is also a melting pot of cultures, enriched by the waves of European immigration over the last two centuries. Our Spanish heritage is the main ingredient.

Our Spanish roots no doubt explain the culinary time clock of the Argentinean day. Any native of Madrid or Barcelona would recognize it instantly. We begin with a simple light breakfast of rolls and coffee. Our ideal lunch might be a rib eye with a fresh green salad and French fries, and a hearty Malbec from Mendoza. After such a generous meal, we still have the tradition of the afternoon siesta. How I love smoking a cigar after lunch,

OPPOSITE: Lago la Plata, the so-called silver lake of Patagonia, where I built my family cabin.

lying down with a book of poems and some Debussy on my headphones, and then drifting off for a few hours. The march of "progress" has started to interfere with siesta time—but not with mine. I let my BlackBerry buzz away as the messages pile up.

Late afternoons are for work again. Cocktail hour is no earlier than eight or nine o'clock. As in Spain, dinner in Argentina is never early. If you show up at a restaurant at nine, you are considered an early bird. It's much more common to gather at ten or ten-thirty, and, even for children, midnight is not an unusual time to sit down to eat. There is something elegant and sophisticated about an Argentinean restaurant late at night. The women all look ravishing in their cocktail dresses, with their hair done just so and their jewelry reflecting the candlelight. The men, too, are natty and well turned out, as if ready to ask their lovely dinner partners to join them in a sultry tango on the dance floor. Eating so late means we get to bed later, which is another reason that an afternoon siesta is welcome.

However, Spain is not our only influence. Many of the vast movements of immigrants that reached the United States and Canada also affected Argentina. Our biggest influx was from Italy. In fact, if you listen to the accent of natives of Buenos Aires, the Spanish has a very Italian intonation to it—almost a melody. There are Italian bak-

eries all over the country, as well as fresh pasta stores. Garlic, fresh herbs, lemon juice, and olive oil are as common to Argentinean food as they are to the Italian table.

There was also a great wave of German immigration in the nineteenth century; my ancestors, who arrived in the 1880s, were part of that. The pancakes, apple tarts, and dark breads of the mountain towns in the western parts of the country have a recognizable German accent.

The Irish, driven from their homeland by famine and politics, brought their love of potatoes with them. (Actually, since the potato is originally native to the Andes, it would be better to say that the Irish brought their potatoes back home.) In some remote mountain valleys in Patagonia, Gaelic is still spoken.

The Spanish also brought the food traditions that they inherited from the Muslims and Jews with whom they shared their homeland for nearly a thousand years. Then, in the last century, many Lebanese and Eastern European Jews arrived in Argentina.

Geographically, Argentina is a long thin country. It is nearly 900 miles at its widest and stretches 2,100 miles from north to south. The majestic Andes run the whole length of our country.

In the north, the high deserts of Salta and the lush vineyards of Mendoza have melded the food traditions of the Incas and the Spanish conquerors. The Malbec grape, which is the foundation of our wine industry, was introduced to Argentina by a Frenchman, but our leading wine-making families are mainly of Italian descent.

In the northeast, we find the wetlands and rain forests of the area we call Mesopotamia (from the Greek for "between the rivers"). Here the native peoples passed down their distinctive fish stews and our national drink, *mate* (MAH-tay), made from the dried leaves of the yerba plant and loved by all. The warm fertile soil of Mesopotamia produces the most marvelous oranges, tangerines, grapefruits, mangoes, and papayas.

Uruguay lies just over the border from these eastern lands. Although legally distinct from Argentina, it's also part of a cultural continuum, and my roots (on my mother's side) are as much Uruguayan as they are Argentine. The world-famous ocean resort of Punta del Este is directly across the Río de la Plata from Buenos Aires. It is our Rivieria and our Hamptons.

The rich plains known as the pampas are the grassy eastern heartland of our country. They are Argentina's granary (with wheat in abundance) and cattle country par excellence. The pampas gave rise to the culture of our iconic cowboy—the saddle-weary gaucho, with his Clint Eastwood scowl and his proudly borne knife scars. Wherever you go in Argentina and Uruguay, you still see gauchos, trotting along on their horses, with sheepskin

saddle blankets, and always trailed by their pack of work dogs, who are always so friendly, even to strangers.

The gauchos developed the open fires of the Argentine barbecue or *parrilla,* the source and inspiration of so many of the recipes in this book. When we gather at a cookout, the fine points of grilling are discussed as heatedly, and with as many differing opinions, as soccer, golf, or polo, all of which are national obsessions.

At the edge of this sea of grassy plains is our capital, Buenos Aires. With its beautiful belle époque architecture and vast leafy parks, *porteños* (people of the port city) think of B.A. as Paris on the river Plata. It is a vibrant, sophisticated metropolis: a city of cafés, bars, dance halls, and restaurants introduced to the world by the incandescent prose of the most famous habitué of those cafés, Jorge Luis Borges. It is a city you can lose your heart to, full of life and larger than life.

To the west and south is remote Patagonia, the tip of the Americas. In its green mountain valleys we grow apples, peaches, pears, plums, and berries. The more arid hillsides and lowlands are perfectly suited to sheepherding, which explains why so many Basque and Welsh immigrants found their way here. To this day, there are plenty of redheaded Joneses all over the region.

In the high valleys, the Andean condor, the world's largest bird, circles overhead, casting a shadow as large as an airplane's. People often say that Patagonia

**LEFT TO RIGHT:** The vines of Mendoza were brought by the French. My favorite vintage cigars, Armagnac, and hat at my cabin in Patagonia. A timeless scene of a gaucho in the mountains. To serve *mate,* our national drink, we use a special spoon and cup.

reminds them of what the American West must have been like a century ago. In fact, with the closing of the American frontier, at the dawn of the twentieth century, Butch Cassidy and the Sundance Kid moved their bank-robbing business here.

When Charles Darwin contemplated Patagonia on his voyages of scientific discovery, he referred to it as "this cursed land." How wrong he was! If you were to look to one place to find the wild authentic heart of Argentina, it would be Patagonia. Although I have lived all over the country, I think of myself first as a son of Patagonia. In the lore of its native peoples, fire was originally the property of the animals: the little armadillo, the nimble Patagonian rabbit, and the ferocious puma. When the wily humans stole the secret of fire, they were careful to guard it, never letting their fires burn out and never sharing them with outsiders. In this book, however, there are no secrets, simply my desire to share.

# The Ways of Fires

Cooking with wood fire is like going on a first date. It is something that you look forward to with great anticipation and a little anxiety. You can never know exactly what the conditions will be: the day can be windy or cold, the wood may be seasoned or green. In a way, every time you cook over wood outdoors, you are starting fresh in a strange kitchen. Once you have done it enough, however, you will always be able to adapt.

## It Starts with Wood

Always use hardwood. In Argentina and Uruguay, I am partial to quebracho, coronilla, and lenga. In North America, oak makes the best coals. Maple is also good, as are birch and hickory. The smoke of the wood of fruit trees adds a whiff of flavoring. Fast-burning hardwoods such as ash don't work as well, and all softwoods (pine, fir, and other evergreens) produce a resinous smoke that ruins the taste of food.

## Where to Build Your Fire

Keep well away from buildings, flammable materials, overhanging branches, etc. A flat dry area will do: look for an even surface of earth, sand, or flat rock. Do not build a fire on your patio, paved driveway, or lawn because it can damage them or, at the very least, mar their appearance.

A ring of large stones or a prefabricated metal fire ring (see photograph opposite) helps to secure the area of your fire, protects it from wind, and focuses the heat.

OPPOSITE: Although a ring of stones or logs will work well, a sturdy cast-iron ring helps contain a fire and reflect heat.

### SAFETY

To deal with occasional flare-ups or swirling embers and to keep the fire from spreading out of control, always have water on hand, as well as a shovel and some dirt, or a fire extinguisher to smother and tamp down any wayward flames. Never use water on a grease fire.

## Light Your Fire

Take note of the wind direction. The dining area should be upwind of the fire; i.e., smoke should blow away from you. You also want to keep your ingredients out of the path of billowing smoke, which can give food a bitter, acrid taste.

» Pile up a few handfuls of wood chips (or ball up a sheet of newspaper).

» Create a tepee of small twigs around the wood chips or paper.

» Create a second tepee of larger twigs, small branches, or split kindling around the first.

» Roll up four or five pieces of newspaper and carefully stick them through the openings in the tepee.

» Create a final tepee of split logs about 4 or 5 inches thick and at least 16 inches long.

» Light the rolled-up newspaper and leave the fire undisturbed until the split logs are ablaze.

» When the fire is well lit, you may begin to add whole round segments of logs, 6 to 9 inches in diameter and not less than 16 inches long.

» For a relatively quick-cooking recipe, such as a steak, you will probably not need to add more wood to your fire. For longer-cooking recipes, you may need to add a dozen or more additional logs.

## From Fire to Coals

Fire is used as a source of coals, which you then shovel or rake under or around your cooking surface, continuing to add more coals as needed during the course of cooking.

I often make use of a "fire basket" placed alongside the cooking grate, in which logs are burned so that the large pieces of glowing coals used for cooking fall through the spaces in the bottom of the basket (see photograph). If you don't have a basket, you can easily use a shovel to move coals from your campfire.

Just as you can turn up the heat or lower it on your stove or in your oven, you can also control the amount of heat that you use in wood-fire cookery. You can move your coals closer to or farther from the grate, pan, or pot. You can raise the grate, move the pot, or arrange the coals in a wood-fired oven so that there are some areas that have a heaping pile of hot coals while other areas have just a thin bed of glowing embers. *In no case should flame ever come into direct contact with ingredients. Flame will overcarbonize ingredients and the result never tastes good.*

## The Life of a Fire:
### Flames, Coals, Embers, Ashes, Cinders

Throughout this book I often refer to coals, embers, and ashes. When you make a wood fire, you rarely cook over direct flame. Instead, you wait for the logs to burn and break up into red-hot coals. After a while those coals will cover over with whitish ash. Then it's the optimum state for cooking. As the coals break down further, from big chunks to smaller glowing pieces, they become embers. And as those embers die down, they cover over with more and more whitish ash until the fire has gone out completely but there is still warmth. Finally all that remains are cold cinders.

### ORGANIZING YOUR WORK SPACE

Before you start your fire, take the time to get your equipment in order. Although this is true any time you cook, it's doubly important when you plan to cook on a fire away from your home kitchen. To set up your grill area, organize wood and tools, including shovel, coal rake or hoe, and fireplace poker or tongs for moving burning wood. Gather other equipment, such as a large wooden carving board, cutting boards, assorted knives, a carving set (knife and large fork), long kitchen tongs, fireproof oven mitts, a spray bottle filled with water to tamp down flames, an instant-read thermometer, a timer, paper towels, and serving platters. For a more complete list, see Sources (page 264).

### WHERE THERE'S FIRE, THERE'S SMOKE

Cooking with wood fire will produce a fair amount of smoke. And even without the wood fire, many of the high-heat recipes in this book make lots of it (especially those that involve burning sugar). If you don't have a strong ventilation fan in the kitchen, save your smoky high-heat grilling for the outdoor grill.

A wrought-iron basket lets the coals fall through at the perfect time to add to the cooking fire.

## How Hot?

The ability to judge the temperature of a fire is something that develops with experience. Until that time, you can use the following rough guide to determine how hot your cooking fire is.

Hold your hand over the coals at about the same distance from the cooking surface as the item you are cooking. Then count the seconds by saying aloud "one Mississippi, two Mississippi . . .," etc. (each whole count is about one second), until you have to remove your hand because it's just to hot. If, for instance, you can count to "five Mississippi," or five seconds, before you pull your hand away, the fire is at medium heat.

| | |
|---|---|
| 2 seconds | High heat |
| 3–4 seconds | Medium-high heat |
| 5–6 seconds | Medium heat |
| 7–8 seconds | Low heat |

The general rule of thumb for meats is the thinner the piece, the more quickly it should cook and, therefore, the higher the heat at which it can cook.

## If You Cook with Charcoal

Figure half as much charcoal, by volume, as wood. Five pounds is the minimum amount of charcoal to create enough coals to cook even the shortest recipe. For a recipe that takes 2 to 3 hours over the fire, I figure twenty pounds of charcoal.

# Parrilla

I believe that the ability to cook meat over a wood fire is inborn in all of us. But perfecting your sixth sense for grilling—knowing exactly when to turn a bone-in rib roast, or precisely how much heat is required to develop a delicious, salty crust on a steak—takes time. It's a skill perfected over the course of hundreds of Sundays conducting a backyard symphony of meat and heat. A great grill master combines skill with acute intuition.

While you can make superb fish, fowl, fruits, and vegetables on the *parrilla*, the true test of an *asador* (grill master) is meat.

It is an article of faith among Argentines that you can never prepare too much meat. People from other countries often are amazed at the amount of meat that we eat (we usually figure 4 pounds per person). The fact is that at every *asado* I have ever been to, people stay for hours and eat until all the meat is gone.

**DEFINITION:** A *parrilla* is a cast-iron barbecue grate set over hot coals.From a hibachi to a Weber-style kettle or a top-of-the-line Viking gas grill, anything with a grate over direct heat can serve as a *parrilla*. A simple grate propped on rocks, cinder blocks, or fireproof bricks will work too.

**DIMENSIONS:** *Parrillas* come in all sizes. If you are having one made, it should be about 36 by 30 inches welded to legs 9 inches high. I like this size because it has ample cooking surface for big family affairs. The added area also means you have the ability to heap coals or spread them out in order to vary heat.

Prepare a bed of coals 4 to 5 inches deep for cooking. This means the grate is about 4 inches above the coals.

**AHEAD OF TIME:** Begin your fire about 45 minutes before you plan to cook. Allow a layer of white ash to completely cover the bed of hot coals. Replenish coals under the grate from a fire alongside the *parrilla*.

**INDOOR ALTERNATIVE:** For all but the largest cuts of meat, use a deep-ridged cast-iron grill pan on a well-ventilated stove.

**OPPOSITE:** Slow-cooked crisped sweetbreads with salt and lemon juice are one of my very favorite *parrilla* dishes.

# Chapa

I love the *chapa* for quick cooking. It produces a crust without drying out the ingredients, so that they stay moist and flavorful. While this method works very well with a thin, quick-cooking steak or a smashed lamb chop, with lower heat you can cook a bigger piece of meat for a longer time; I've made many rib roasts on the *chapa* and they always have a nice crunchy, salty brown crust and tender succulent meat inside.

**DEFINITION:** A *chapa* is a flat piece of cast iron set over a fire. Alternatively, you can use a cast-iron skillet or griddle placed over a barbecue grate, which is in turn placed over a wood, charcoal, or gas fire.

**DIMENSIONS:** A good size for a *chapa* is 30 inches square on legs 12 to 15 inches high. This gives plenty of surface area and enough clearance to make a quick, hot fire with kindling wood and small branches.

**AHEAD OF TIME:** You can heat up a *chapa* quite quickly. A strong kindling wood blaze can be ready to cook within 10 minutes. A drop of water will sizzle and evaporate instantly on a *chapa* over high heat.

**INDOOR ALTERNATIVE:** A cast-iron skillet or griddle on a stove top.

*Chapa* translates as "a piece of sheet metal," but in this book *chapa* cooking means any kind of cooking done on a flat cast-iron surface or griddle. In a way, a *chapa* is a shelter for a fire, a "roof over its head." It's the method that I use the most often in the recipes in this book.

**OPPOSITE:** Thick cast iron set over a fire gives even overall heat. Be careful when you wipe it down with oil, which sometimes causes dramatic flare-ups.

# Infiernillo

Although *infiernillo* is literally translated as "small inferno," I prefer to call this technique "little hell"; it's more poetic. My *infiernillo* is based on the principle that if one fire is good, two fires are better. This method of cooking is especially well suited to preparing meals for large numbers of people. I have fed three hundred people with a half dozen large salmon cooked on a group of *infiernillos*. I was inspired to create this device by the Incas, who use a stone version in the high deserts on the eastern slope of the Andes.

**DEFINITION:** Two fires with a cooking level in between. *Infiernillo* is used primarily for baking large pieces of meat, whole fish, and poultry encased in salt.

**DIMENSIONS:** After years of trial and error, my *infiernillos* are now made of cast iron and measure approximately 36 by 27 inches; the lower level has a 12-inch clearance while the second level has a 20-inch clearance.

**OUTDOOR ALTERNATIVE:** Use two pieces of sheet metal or two griddles set on cinder blocks, rocks, or bricks.

**INDOOR ALTERNATIVE:** When cooking in a salt crust, use a home oven turned to its highest temperature.

**OPPOSITE:** The intense overall heat of the two fires of an *infiernillo* diffused through a salt crust is surprisingly gentle on delicate ingredients such as fish.

# Horno de Barro

For most wood-oven cooking, I make a fire in the back of the oven where it will reflect the most heat. Although some chefs remove the firewood when the oven reaches the desired temperature, I prefer to keep the fire going until it has burned itself out, because the radiant heat adds something. You can raise heat for long-cooking recipes by adding more wood to your fire. Small pieces of wood that catch fire quickly will bring up the temperature quickly. As for lowering the heat, it is a long and gradual process that the chef does not have much control over; moving whatever you are cooking farther from the hotter back wall will have some effect.

**DEFINITION:** The *horno de barro* is similar to the outdoor bread ovens that I remember from my time working in the kitchens of Tuscany. I keep mine going all through the day, using it to cook at high heat and then, as it cools down, to bake breads and pies. It's quite a project to build an oven, but luckily they can be bought ready-made (see Sources, page 264).

**AHEAD OF TIME:** Start your fire about 1 hour before you are ready to cook at high heat. Wait for the lining of the oven to turn whitish from the heat and ashes.

**TEMPERATURE CONTROL:** Although I heat my ovens in excess of 1000°F, none of the recipes in this book need to be made at a temperature over 500°F. As you learn to be comfortable with your wood oven, you can experiment with raising the temperature. An infrared oven thermometer is invaluable (see Sources, page 264) in

**OPPOSITE:** My wood-burning ovens are used twenty-four hours a day. The closer you place your pans and ingredients to the rear, the more intense the heat.

helping you master this oven and the art of maintaining its temperature. Keep in mind that all wood ovens vary, as do all woods—so the best teacher here is time and experience.

**INDOOR ALTERNATIVE:** A conventional home oven.

Some say we inherited our outdoor ovens from the Incas, while others point to the dome-shaped ovens that the Moors brought to Spain. I think it's probably the off-spring of a marriage between Old World and New.

I was introduced to the *horno* by one of my early mentors in fire cookery, Fernando Lecuona. A great bon vivant and culinary historian, Fernando was an amateur chef in Salta, a province where they still follow the old traditions of cooking. His history of Salteño cuisine is one of my cooking bibles.

# Rescoldo

If you have ever put a hot potato in the embers and covered it with ashes, you already know the *rescoldo* method. Before the arrival of the Spaniards, this style of cooking was favored by the Ona Indians, who still live in the far south of Patagonia and on Tierra del Fuego. The Onas would cook the huge eggs of the native ostrich as well as the bountiful shellfish found off the coast *rescoldo*-style. They kept glowing embers, hot ashes, and fire-warmed rocks in their canoes, so that they could even cook while afloat.

Like country folk all over the world, the Indians of Argentina believed that nothing should be wasted. This includes fire—as long as it can be used for cooking, one should use it. The even, gentle heat of a bed of cinders can't be beat for all kinds of vegetables: whole pumpkins, sweet potatoes, bell peppers, corn in the husk. This is the essence of *rescoldo*—capturing every last bit of cookable warmth from a slowly dying fire.

**DEFINITION:** *Rescoldo* is a method of cooking by covering ingredients with hot embers and warm ashes.

**AHEAD OF TIME:** Always use hot embers and ashes, not big pieces of red hot coals. If you start your fire 1 hour ahead of time, you should have enough. *Rescoldo* is usually done as an additional use for any cooking fire. In other words, if you are cooking over a *parrilla*, make your *rescoldo* with some of the embers and ashes used for preparing the coals for the *parrilla*.

**INDOOR ALTERNATIVE:** A home fireplace.

**OPPOSITE:** Part of the beauty of cooking in a bed of embers and ashes is that there's no fuss required: first you cover the ingredient, then you wait, then you uncover it. The magic takes place out of sight.

# Asador

Some years ago I was preparing a whole lamb *al asador* at one of the most elegant *grand crus* châteaux of France. When the owner saw me doing this, he jumped up and exclaimed, *"Ca, c'est des Arabes!"* He was right: this dramatic way of slowly roasting a lamb came to Spain and the rest of Europe from the Arab world, where it is called a *mechoui*. Today, all through Patagonia, where shepherding is the principal industry, a whole roast lamb is as common as a standing rib roast or a stuffed turkey is in the United States. It's dramatic and it feeds a lot of people.

**DEFINITION:** *Asador* is a method for cooking whole animals—pig, lamb, or goat—which are butterflied and fastened with wires (and sometimes hooks) to an iron cross with two crosspieces.

**DIMENSIONS:** To accommodate whole animals, you will need a 6-foot-long piece of iron, pointed at one end (for insertion into the ground), and two crosspieces, which are welded to the vertical piece. The upper crosspiece should be 31 inches long and the bottom one 24 inches; hooks are optional.

**AHEAD OF TIME:** Start a fire 1½ to 2 hours before you are ready to cook. You will need about 10 round logs to begin and at least another 15 to 20 to keep the fire going for 4 to 6 hours.

**TEMPERATURE CONTROL:** Vary the amount of heat by leaning the cross toward or away from the fire. In the last stages of cooking, I take coals and embers from the fire and spread them under the bottom of the meat to provide more slow-cooking heat as needed.

*Todo bicho que camina
va a parar al asador.*

Every creature that walks
ends up roasting on the iron cross.

—OLD ARGENTINE PROVERB

**OPPOSITE:** A whole lamb roasted before an open fire is an ever-present sign of our Basque heritage.

# Caldero

Every *estancia*, or ranch, has some version of a *caldero:* a big iron pot, usually a very big iron pot to feed large groups. It is not uncommon to find a *caldero* that has been in the same family since the days of the founder of the ranch. If an open fire with a simple grill symbolizes the lonely independent life of our gauchos out on the vast pampas, then a huge *caldero,* one capable of holding a hundred gallons of stew, is the symbol of the life at the center of the *estancia*.

**DEFINITION:** A *caldero* is a large cast-iron kettle or Dutch oven. For boiling water or gentle heating, you may place a caldero directly on top of a *parrilla* or *chapa*.

**TEMPERATURE CONTROL:** To adjust heat, simply move the *caldero* closer to or farther away from the fire or coals (this won't be possible with very large *calderos*, like the one pictured opposite). You may also rest the *caldero* on a bed of coals or ashes.

**INDOOR ALTERNATIVE:** A cast-iron cauldron or Dutch oven. Although we use vessels up to 100 gallons for ranch meals, a 5- or 7-quart Dutch oven will serve for most families and cookouts.

**SAFETY NOTE:** When using a *caldero* for deep-frying, fill it no more than halfway. Be careful not to spatter oil, which can cause dangerous flare-ups. A spatter screen (see Sources, page 264) is a good idea for extra safety.

**CARING FOR YOUR CALDERO:** Some recipes call for cooking with wine (such as 7½-Hour Lamb Malbec with Rosemary and Lemon, page 114), and others use ingredients that are acidic in themselves (for instance, Tomato and Bread Soup with Poached Eggs, page 195). Cast iron might discolor ingredients, but it does no harm (in fact, it adds nutrition). You can give your *caldero* an extra coat or two of seasoning by frying up a couple of batches of potatoes or chicken. This will set the seasoning more fully and make discoloration less likely.

**OPPOSITE:** This *caldero* is typical of the giant ones you still can see on the *estancias* out on the pampas, where they are handed down from generation to generation.

# The First Commandment—Don't Touch!

Patience is a virtue in and out of the kitchen, whether it's waiting six hours for dough to rise or four years until someone you have admired from afar finally notices that your interest is more than passing. Cooking is about waiting.

If there is one unbreakable rule that puts patience to the test it is this: when working with high heat, the first contact between the cooking surface and the food must be respected.

You must wait . . .

Leave it alone . . .

Don't touch it . . .

Don't move it . . .

And, above all, don't flip it.

Why?

Because anything that contains protein, starch, or sugar is capable of building up a crust and of all the delights of the palate, nothing signals pleasure more than the crunch of a crust and the taste of caramelized and crisped bits. Think of a steak without a seared salty crust, fried potatoes that aren't crispy, or pizza without any of those little charred areas on the bottom—all of these wonderful foods become insipid and uninteresting without that crust. Crust concentrates the taste of everything you cook.

This seems like a simple enough principle, but there's something about food on the fire or in the skillet that makes people want to move it and flip it. Resist this impulse! Flip it only once. Other than that, don't move it, or you'll rupture the protective coating of flavor-enhancing and moisture-sealing crust that's created when food comes into contact with heat. That first encounter between food and heat is like a first kiss: it happens only once.

So how long should you wait before moving the food? These recipes will serve as guidelines, but they're not commandments. Every piece of wood, every piece of meat, and every cooking surface varies, and you have to learn to adapt. With time, you'll recognize the clues that food always gives you—the first wafts of charring, the bubbling of liquid weeping out of a tomato, the brown edges of a crepe as it defines its shape—and you'll know when it's time to turn your food or remove it from the heat. Flip it too quickly, and you won't have a crust. But wait too long and you'll have a black, overly burnt result. While I love the taste of burnt, its elegance comes from just having some charring, not incineration.

So, if something doesn't land precisely on the perfect spot of your skillet, leave it be! Heat and time will do their work: moving it will only add another misstep.

When in doubt . . . don't!

I've cooked with the most beautiful gleaming copper pots and pans and with lovely enameled French cookware of every size and description, but if I had to pick one material for its all-around utility, it would be endlessly versatile cast iron. It's no accident that gauchos, campers, hunters, and explorers always find a way to include a cast-iron skillet in their kit. Nothing transfers the heat of a fire more uniformly, and nothing stands up to the massive heat of a wood oven or bonfire better. Because of its thickness, cast iron retains heat for a long time. If you use a ridged grill pan, you can nearly duplicate the crosshatching effect achieved with steaks and chops on an outdoor grill.

I depend on cast iron, and I respect it, but I don't go through the elaborate steps that some aficionados do when cleaning it. I know that many people never wash their cast-iron pans with soap and water, scouring them instead with coarse salt, then oiling the pans to develop a nonstick patina that's equal to Teflon. I'm not one of them. I find that a pan that is oil-seasoned often smokes excessively while it's heating up; I prefer to oil my ingredients just before putting them on to cook. As far as cleaning off the sticky bits, pouring boiling water into a pan or dousing a very hot pan or skillet with a ladleful of warm water shocks them so you can easily scrape them off with a big spoon, spatula, or—my favorite *chapa* tool—a wide putty knife (the kind used by housepainters and plasterers; see page 224).

I confess that my pans often show rust, and some even crack from time to time, but I just chalk that up to paying my dues.

# Appetizers

I fell in love with these banquettes when I saw them in an Ingmar Bergman
movie. I have them in all my homes and restaurants.

Nothing wakes up the appetite quite like food cooking over an open fire. Most of the appetizers in this chapter are hot ones, but we begin with a selection of four palate teasers that can be served while waiting for the fire. That's because people always want a little something to go with a glass of wine as they watch the drama unfold.

# Zucchini with Basil, Mint, and Parmesan

Very fresh tasting and light. If you have small leaves of basil and mint, use them whole; otherwise, roughly tear them. This recipe can be doubled, tripled, or further multiplied. And it can be made several hours ahead.

| Serves 4

1 good-sized zucchini, trimmed

1 lemon

2 tablespoons chipped or shaved Parmesan

Coarse salt and freshly ground black pepper

2 tablespoons extra virgin olive oil

10 small fresh basil leaves

10 small fresh mint leaves

Sliced baguette, toasted if desired

With a mandoline or a sharp knife, slice the zucchini on an angle into long ovals about $1/16$ inch thick. Place in a bowl.

Grate the zest of half the lemon over the zucchini, and squeeze all the juice over it.

Add the Parmesan to the zucchini. Season carefully with salt and pepper. Toss with the olive oil, basil, and mint. (The zucchini can be refrigerated for up to 3 hours; if you do refrigerate it, don't add the basil and mint until just before you offer it.) Serve with slices of baguette.

# Pears and Ibérico Ham with Parsley, Olive Oil, and Garlic Sauce

The silky-textured long-cured flesh of the Ibérico hog, fattened on sweet, nutty acorns, is one of the glories of global gastronomy. Here, the ham, perfectly balanced by the fruity, acidic pear, has enough flavor to stand up to the combination of garlic, parsley, and olive oil.

| Serves 4 to 6

2 ripe pears, about 9 ounces each

Freshly ground black pepper

2 tablespoons extra virgin olive oil

4 ounces thinly sliced *jamón ibérico* or other
    top-quality air-dried ham, such as serrano
    or prosciutto

Unsalted butter, at room temperature

1 baguette, sliced

1/4 cup Parsley, Olive Oil, and Garlic Sauce
    (page 252)

Cut the pears in half, core them, and slice lengthwise $1/8$ inch thick. Sprinkle with pepper and the extra virgin olive oil.

Cut the ham into pieces about the same size as the pear slices. Butter the sliced baguette.

Working in overlapping circles from the outside in, lay down slices of pear interspersed with slices of ham on a serving platter so that you end up with a flower-like pattern. Drizzle with the sauce and serve with the buttered slices of baguette.

# Fresh Figs with Mozzarella, Thyme, and Olive Oil

One of the most popular starters at all of my restaurants. It's important that the figs and the mozzarella be torn rather than cut—the rustic-looking result fits the unfussy ambience of the fireside. Thyme, which is usually used to enhance savory ingredients, adds a wonderful counterpoint to the sweet, fruity figs.

| Serves 8 to 12

**20 fresh figs**
**12 ounces mozzarella di bufala**
**Coarse salt and freshly ground black pepper**
**2 tablespoons fresh thyme leaves**
**Best-quality extra virgin olive oil**
**Crusty bread**

Tear the figs in half and arrange about an inch apart on a large serving platter. Tear the mozzarella into pieces about the same size as the figs and arrange in between and around the figs. Season to taste with salt and pepper. Scatter the thyme leaves over all and drizzle with olive oil.

    Serve with crusty bread.

# Endives, Sun-Dried Tomatoes, and Olives

There are many levels of bitterness in this bracing appetizer—in the lemon zest, the olives, the thyme, and, of course, the endives—but it is nuanced and never overpowering. It keeps the taste bright, clean, and is especially well balanced by the wafer-thin sun-dried tomatoes (you'll find these are much more delicate and fruity than the oil-soaked store-bought variety). | Serves 8

**1 cup Sun-Dried Tomatoes (page 254), minced**
**½ cup pitted and minced Kalamata olives**
**1 teaspoon minced lemon zest**
**1 tablespoon minced fresh thyme leaves**
**½ cup extra virgin olive oil**
**Coarse salt and freshly ground black pepper**
**8 endives**

Combine the tomatoes, olives, lemon zest, and thyme in a bowl. Add the olive oil and toss. Season to taste with salt and pepper.

    Trim and wash the endives and dry with paper towels. Separate the leaves. Place a teaspoonful of the tomato mixture in each endive leaf and arrange on a large serving platter.

# Burnt Tomato, Goat Cheese, and Anchovy Bruschetta

Whenever I make bruschetta, I think of Aldo Langhi, chef of La Cave di Maiano, a restaurant in the hillside town of Fiesole outside Florence. Aldo's good nature no doubt had something to do with my affection for his food. Somehow, even at the frantic height of tourist season, calm reigned, and the result was impeccable food. Over the years, many of my cooks have spent a few months with Aldo, learning his cooking secrets, but also learning how to be both efficient and peaceful in a restaurant kitchen.

This recipe is my way of paying respect to a master of simple bruschetta. The key is the burning of the tomatoes. By blackening the cut sides to a crust, you get toasty bitterness and then a beautiful release of sweet tomato water when you bite down. The anchovies add pungency and the goat cheese smooths it all out. | Serves 8

36 cherry tomatoes (about 1 pound)
½ cup fresh oregano leaves
¼ cup extra virgin olive oil
Coarse salt and freshly ground black pepper
1 day-old baguette (10 ounces) sliced into twenty-
 four ½-inch-thick rounds, toasted until crisp
8 ounces Bûcheron or similar goat cheese
24 anchovy fillets (about 3½ ounces), drained and
 halved lengthwise
Parsley, Olive Oil, and Garlic Sauce (page 252)

Cut the tomatoes in half and put them in a bowl. Add the oregano, olive oil, and salt and pepper to taste. Toss to combine.

Heat a *chapa* or large cast-iron griddle over very high heat. When it is very hot, place the cherry tomato halves cut side down about 1 inch apart on the hot surface; work in batches if necessary. It is very important not to move the tomatoes while they cook, or they will release their juices and lose their shape and texture. Keep in mind that it is hard to char a tomato too much: best to err on the side of charring; and if you do move one, you are committed and you should remove it immediately. When you see that the tomatoes are well charred on the bottom, almost black (about 4 minutes), remove them using tongs or a spatula and place burnt side up on a large tray, about an inch apart so they don't steam.

Arrange the toasted bread rounds on a platter. Spread some of the goat cheese on each round, and place 3 tomato halves on top of the cheese. Garnish with the anchovies and drizzle a teaspoonful of the sauce on top. Serve immediately.

Photograph on page 39

# Burnt Ricotta Salata, Tomatoes, and Olives

Some years ago I drove to the lovely city of Arezzo with my son, Francisco, to see *The Dream of Constantine,* by my favorite Renaissance painter, Piero della Francesca. While waiting for the church that housed the painting to reopen after lunch—always a gamble in Italy, no matter what the sign says—we had a memorable lunch at Il Pescatore featuring a version of this salad followed by a grilled fish and chicory. Nine-year-old Francisco found it somewhat of an ordeal, especially since the poor boy had to wear a tie. He looked at me and asked, "Papa, can we go to McDonald's?"

This classic Italian combination gets a New World twist with the addition of fresh chile. | Serves 6

1 teaspoon sugar

3 tablespoons red wine vinegar

½ cup extra virgin olive oil

½ cup fresh oregano leaves

12 ounces cherry tomatoes, cut in half

1 cup Kalamata olives

10 ounces ricotta salata

2 small red chiles

Coarse salt

¼ teaspoon crushed red pepper flakes

Whisk together the sugar, red wine vinegar, 3 tablespoons of the olive oil, and the oregano in a bowl. Add the tomatoes and toss to coat.

Smash the olives with the side of a heavy knife and tear them open, removing the pits. Toss the olives and tomatoes together on a serving platter.

Break the ricotta salata into rough 1-inch pieces and place in a bowl. Halve the chiles, remove the seeds, and cut lengthwise into thin slices. Add to the ricotta, and toss with the remaining 5 tablespoons olive oil.

Heat a *chapa* or large cast-iron skillet over high heat. Add the ricotta and chiles in batches, so they aren't crowded, and cook without moving for 5 to 10 seconds: as soon as you see the cheese charring on the bottom, remove the cheese and chiles and place burnt side up over the tomatoes and olives. Sprinkle with salt and the red pepper flakes. Serve immediately.

OPPOSITE: A table setting at Patagonia Sur, my restaurant in Buenos Aires.
ABOVE: Burnt Tomato, Goat Cheese, and Anchovy Bruschetta (page 36).

# Smashed Beets with Greens, Goat Cheese, and Garlic Chips

The beauty of beets is not apparent when they're boiled into tasteless submission. But if they're cooked in a broth enriched with olive oil and vinegar, then smashed and griddled, their natural sugar content results in a chewy, crunchy burnt crust and soft, sweet insides.

Scrub the beets well with a brush but don't peel them—they are most delicious served with the skin on.

| Serves 8

**8 equal-sized red beets, scrubbed and stems trimmed to 1 inch (reserve the greens)**

**½ cup plus 2 tablespoons red wine vinegar**

**½ cup plus 2 tablespoons extra virgin olive oil, plus a little more for the pan**

**5 black peppercorns**

**2 bay leaves**

**Coarse salt**

**Freshly ground black pepper**

**A large handful of beet greens (reserved from above), trimmed, washed, and dried**

**3 cups mixed greens, arugula, or spinach**

**8 ounces Bûcheron or similar goat cheese**

**Crispy Garlic Chips (page 255), made with 10 garlic cloves and 1 cup oil**

Put the beets in a large saucepan with ½ cup of the vinegar, 2 tablespoons of the olive oil, the peppercorns, bay leaves, and 1 tablespoon salt. Cover with cold water and bring to a boil over high heat. Reduce the heat and boil gently for 25 to 35 minutes, depending on the size of the beets, until they are tender enough to be easily pierced with the tip of a knife. Drain in a colander.

Beets are messy so use paper towels to prevent stains. With the palm of your hand, gently smash the beet between the towels: you want it to yield just enough to flatten slightly but not crumble apart. Use a wide spatula to transfer the beet to a tray lined with foil (for easier cleanup). Repeat with the remaining beets. Brush the beets with 2 tablespoons olive oil and season with salt and pepper.

Brush a *chapa* or large cast-iron skillet with olive oil and heat over high heat. When it is hot enough for a drop of water to sizzle on the surface, add the smashed beets (you may need to do this in two batches) and cook for about 2 minutes on each side, letting them blacken. Transfer the beets to the foil-lined tray and adjust the seasoning if necessary.

To make the vinaigrette, pour the remaining 2 tablespoons vinegar into a small bowl and gradually whisk in the remaining 6 tablespoons olive oil until emulsified. Season to taste with salt and pepper.

To serve, toss the beet greens with the mixed greens and place a mound of greens on each plate. Place the smashed beets alongside the greens and crumble the goat cheese over them. Drizzle with the vinaigrette, and scatter the garlic chips over all.

# Humita

## Savory Corn Pudding

I first encountered *humita,* as it has always been made by native people, in the northern province of Salta. In many ways, I think Salta is the part of my country with the richest culinary traditions. Many of the Indians there speak Quechua, the ancient Inca language, and the women mill their corn by pounding it on rocks that have been worn down over the centuries. The *señores* still come to lunch with their guns tucked into their belts!

The traditional *humita* is prepared and served in corn husks, but I find that this recipe is simpler and fresher. The most important thing to keep in mind is that you must do it only when corn is sweet and just picked at the peak of the season. Grate it rather than cut it off the cob. Only then will it release the sweet juice that mingles so well with the spicy red pepper flakes, onion, and fresh basil. Serve with toasted country bread and a green salad. | Serves 4

8 ears corn, preferably yellow, as fresh and sweet
    as possible, husks removed
2 tablespoons unsalted butter
1 tablespoon extra virgin olive oil
1 cup chopped onion
½ cup whole milk
1 cup fresh basil leaves
1 teaspoon crushed red pepper flakes, or to taste
Coarse salt
1 teaspoon sugar (optional)

Using a box grater, grate the corn kernels into a large bowl. Then run the back of a knife down each cob to release all the milky liquid from the kernels.

Melt the butter with the olive oil in a *caldero* or Dutch oven over medium-low heat. Add the onion and sauté, stirring, until it is translucent, 8 to 10 minutes; it should not brown. Stir in the corn with all its liquid, and sauté, stirring until the mixture thickens. Stir in ¼ cup of the milk. Once the milk is absorbed, gradually stir in the rest of the milk. Reduce the heat and simmer, stirring, until the corn is creamy, 4 to 5 minutes, depending on the size and freshness of the corn.

Chop the basil and add it to the corn, along with the crushed red pepper flakes, salt, and sugar, if desired.

# Butternut Squash Soup
# with Garlic and White Wine

I included this recipe in my first book, *Frio, Tibio, Caliente (Cold, Warm, Hot)* and I still make it. It is creamy in texture, although there is no cream in it, and the flavors of the squash and the wine intensify and deepen each other. I have a theory about soup: by the third mouthful, most people are bored, even with the most delicious soup. Add a little crunch, however, and it stays interesting. | Serves 6 to 8

1 large butternut squash, about 3½ pounds
4 tablespoons unsalted butter
2 tablespoons extra virgin olive oil
2 large onions, thinly sliced
4 large garlic cloves, smashed and peeled
¾ cup dry white wine
2 tablespoons fresh thyme leaves
Coarse salt and coarsely ground black pepper
4 cups vegetable stock
6 to 8 thin slices of crisp toasted Pan de Campo
    (page 243), or Toasted Fresh Bread Crumbs
    (page 254)
Freshly grated Parmesan for garnish

Peel and halve the butternut squash. Discard the seeds and fibrous center, and cut into 1½-inch cubes.

Heat the butter and olive oil in a *caldero* or Dutch oven over medium heat. Add the onions and garlic and sauté, stirring occasionally, until soft and golden, about 10 minutes. Add the squash and stir to combine, then add the white wine, 1 generous tablespoon thyme, and salt and pepper to taste. Raise the heat and cook for about 5 minutes, until the wine has evaporated. Add the stock (it should just cover the vegetables) and bring to a boil. Reduce the heat to low and cook gently, uncovered, for 20 to 25 minutes, until the squash is very tender.

Puree the soup with an immersion blender (or puree in a regular blender, and reheat if necessary). Adjust the seasoning and ladle into soup bowls. Top each serving with a slice of toast or a generous spoonfull of toasted bread crumbs. Sprinkle with the remaining thyme and fresh Parmesan and serve immediately.

Photograph on page 44

# Burnt Carrots with Goat Cheese, Parsley, Arugula, and Crispy Garlic Chips

Carrots are like a quiet but secretly remarkable child who doesn't attract much attention. Most often they're simply what you throw into a soup or a braised dish to "add a little sweetness." But it's because of that inner sweetness that they're so suited to charring on a *chapa*. The sugar caramelizes and produces a delicious crust. They are tossed with nutty garlic chips, peppery arugula, and creamy goat cheese. | Serves 8

2 tablespoons red wine vinegar
½ cup plus 1 to 2 tablespoons extra virgin olive oil
Coarse salt and freshly ground black pepper
8 medium carrots (about 1¼ pounds), peeled
1 tablespoon chopped fresh thyme
1 small bunch flat-leaf parsley, leaves only
2 bunches arugula, trimmed, washed, and dried
6 ounces Bûcheron or similar goat cheese,
    sliced ½ inch thick
Crispy Garlic Chips (page 255)

To make the vinaigrette, pour the vinegar into a small bowl and whisk in 5 tablespoons of the extra virgin olive oil. Season to taste with salt and pepper. Set aside.

Cut the carrots crosswise in half, then cut the halves into thick rough sticks. Toss in a bowl with 3 tablespoons of the olive oil, the thyme, and salt and pepper to taste.

Heat a *chapa* or large cast-iron skillet over high heat. Working in batches if necessary, add the carrots in a single layer and cook, without turning, until they are charred on the bottom and almost burned, 3 to 5 minutes. Turn with a spatula and cook on the other side for 2 to 3 minutes more, adjusting the heat as necessary, until they are crunchy on the outside and tender within. Transfer to a tray. Wipe out the skillet, if using, and set aside.

Combine the parsley and arugula on a large serving platter and toss lightly with half the vinaigrette. Place the carrots on top.

Reheat the *chapa* or skillet to very high heat and coat with the remaining 1 to 2 tablespoons olive oil. Immediately add the slices of goat cheese: be careful—the oil may spatter. As soon as you see the cheese blacken on the bottom, remove the slices with a thin spatula and invert onto the carrots. Toss the garlic chips over the salad and drizzle with the remaining vinaigrette.

Photograph on page 49

PREVIOUS SPREAD, LEFT: The bar of Francis Mallmann 1884 in Mendoza.
RIGHT: Burnt Carrots with Goat Cheese, Parsley, Arugula, and Crispy
Garlic Chips (page 47).

# Grilled Polenta with
# Burnt Tomatoes and Morcilla

Morcilla, a type of sausage known to Cajuns as *boudin* and the English as blood pudding, has the consistency of tapioca—from plump grains of rice—and the taste of meat, from the congealed blood. The burnt tomatoes are slightly acidic and juicy, and the sweet, starchy corn used to make the cornmeal caramelizes.

Make the burnt tomatoes while the polenta and morcilla cook, so they will be hot when you serve them.

| Serves 8

FOR THE POLENTA

**2 cups milk**

**2 cups water**

**1 tablespoon extra virgin olive oil**

**2 bay leaves**

**2 teaspoons coarse salt**

**1½ teaspoons freshly ground black pepper**

**2 cups quick-cooking fine polenta**

**8 tablespoons (1 stick) unsalted butter,
    at room temperature**

**1 cup freshly grated Parmesan**

**¼ cup small fresh oregano leaves**

**1 pound morcilla sausage**

**Olive oil**

**A double recipe of Burnt Tomato Halves
    (page 181)**

To make the polenta, line a 9-by-12-inch baking pan with plastic wrap. Combine the milk, water, olive oil, bay leaves, salt, and pepper in a wide pot. Stir in the polenta, bring to a boil, and cook, stirring constantly, until the polenta thickens and holds its shape, 5 to 6 minutes. Remove from the heat and beat in the butter by the tablespoon, then beat in the Parmesan. Stir in the oregano.

Spread the polenta in the lined baking pan. Cover the polenta with plastic wrap and use your hands to flatten it evenly. Chill until firm, about 30 minutes.

Meanwhile, with a sharp serrated knife, slice the morcilla into 1-inch pieces—take care to slice with a gentle back-and-forth motion so that you don't force the sausage out of the casing. Set aside.

Cut the chilled polenta into 3-inch squares. Lift the squares out of the pan and cut each one on the diagonal into 2 triangles.

Heat a *chapa* or large cast-iron griddle over high heat until a drop of water sizzles on the surface. Brush with olive oil. Place the polenta triangles on the hot surface, without crowding (work in batches if necessary), and grill for 3 minutes on each side, or until nicely browned. Arrange on a large platter.

Wipe off the hot surface and return to high heat. Add the morcilla and cook until well browned on both sides and cooked through, about 3 minutes on each side. Arrange on the platter with the polenta and the tomatoes. Serve immediately.

The Glorious Empanada

If I had to pick one food that is most typical of Argentina, it would be the crispy fried or baked turnover known as the empanada. People eat these at the start of big meals or make a filling meal-on-the-go out of them. Many times, on the long road trip to my cabin at "the Island" in the most remote part of Patagonia, I have pulled into a little mountain town at midnight—at which time families with small children are still coming in for a big dinner—and

ordered up a paper sack of empanadas. After wolfing down a few, I can continue driving through the night, past the hulking ghostly mass of the volcano they call Lanin—"the Deaf One"—which soars over the moon-lit pampas; a herd of guanacos ford a swift-flowing stream with an Indian name that fills your mouth like a forkful of pasta—Caleufu, Collan Cura, Huaca Muamuil; the silver stars of the Southern Cross stud the blue black sky; and the Rolling Stones blare from the stereo. As dawn drives away the darkness, I contemplate the scene with a last taste of salty, savory empanada while filling the gas tank and ordering some fresh coffee.

Instead of empanada, singular, it would be more proper to say empanadas, because the recipe changes from province to province, from town to town, and often, from household to household. Most have meat; some have olives or eggs or raisins or other additions, others do not. For perfect empanadas, all would agree on a few points:

### HOW TO EAT AN EMPANADA

Children are often told, not to slurp their food. Please disregard this when it comes to empana-das. If you use a good amount of lard or butter in the filling, they'll be very juicy, so you either slurp or end up with a mess. Even a few drops of precious empanada juices on your plate—or on your clothes—is taken as a lack of skill in Salta: a Salteño can eat a whole order of empanadas wearing a white shirt, and it remains spotless!

» For crisp, flaky dough, use lard as your shortening. While you can make empanadas with other shorten-ings, top-quality unhydrogenated lard, unlike more easily available processed lard, has no trans fat, and it makes a light, flaky dough with great depth of flavor. It's often available from heritage pork producers at farmers' markets.

» Always chop the meat by hand, using a sharp knife. Ground meat tends to give up a lot of liquid with the result that the meat ends up boiling in its juices and will be dry and tough. For the same reason, when frying meat for your filling, don't crowd the pan, or the meat will steam, not sear. Let all those little pieces crisp and seal in their juices.

» Should you fry empanadas or bake them? I do both. At cookouts I fry them (by tradition, for about as long as it takes to recite a paternoster—about forty seconds). In my restaurants, I bake them.

The recipes that follow are my two favorite variations, the Mendocina style from the wine country, with olives, and the Salteña, which has potatoes and spicy seasonings.

# Empanadas Mendocinas

| Makes enough for 24 empanadas

FOR THE FILLING

1 pound well-marbled stewing beef,
  such as sirloin tip or triangle (tri-tip)
Coarse salt and freshly ground black pepper
10 tablespoons (1¼ sticks) unsalted butter
¼ cup high-quality lard
3 medium onions, quartered and very thinly sliced
1 tablespoon crushed red pepper flakes
1 tablespoon ground cumin
1 tablespoon *pimentón dulce*
  (sweet Spanish smoked paprika)
4 scallions, minced, white and green parts kept
  separate
2 tablespoons extra virgin olive oil
¼ cup fresh oregano leaves, coarsely chopped
3 hard-boiled large eggs, coarsely chopped
½ cup pitted green olives, coarsely chopped

Empanada Dough (page 57)

Trim and discard any gristle from the meat, but leave the fat. With a sharp knife, chop the meat into ⅛-inch pieces. Transfer the meat to a bowl and season with salt and pepper to taste.

Melt 6 tablespoons of the butter and 1 table-spoon of the lard in a large skillet over medium-low heat. Add the onions and sauté until they are trans-lucent, about 8 minutes; do not allow them to brown. Add the red pepper flakes, cumin, *pimentón,* and the white part of the scallions and sauté for 2 minutes more. Turn off the heat and stir in the scallion greens. Season to taste with salt and black pepper.

Heat the olive oil in a large skillet over high heat. Brown the meat in batches, and spread the browned meat out on a tray, so it doesn't steam. When all the meat is browned, combine in a bowl with the onion mixture, the remaining 3 tablespoons lard, and the oregano. Adjust the seasoning, cover with plastic wrap, and chill until firm. (The filling can be made up to 1 day ahead.)

To assemble and cook the empanadas, cut one piece of dough in half; keep the other half covered with plastic until ready to use. With a rolling pin, roll the dough out on a floured work surface into a rectangle about 8 by 22 inches and ⅛ inch thick or less, or roll through a pasta machine, starting on the widest setting and decreasing settings as you con-tinue until the dough strips are ⅛ inch thick or less. On the floured surface, using a biscuit cutter or a water glass, cut the dough into 3½-inch circles; you should be able to cut 6 circles. Transfer the circles to a floured baking sheet and cover with plastic wrap. Repeat with the remaining dough.

Heat an *horno de barro* or home oven (with the racks positioned in the upper and lower thirds of the oven) to approximately 350°F. Remove the filling from the refrigerator. Oil two large baking sheets.

Cut the remaining 4 tablespoons butter into small pieces, and set out a cup of water.

*To assemble the empanadas the traditional way,* lay a circle of dough in the palm of your hand. Place a heaping tablespoon of filling onto one half of the circle, leaving a ⅓-inch border, and top the filling with a pinch each of chopped egg and chopped olives and a dot of butter. With your finger or a pastry brush, moisten the edges of the dough with water, then fold the dough over the filling in a half-moon shape and pinch the edges together, forming pleats to seal the dough (see photographs, page 57). Transfer to one of the oiled baking sheets. Repeat with the remaining dough circles and filling.

*Alternatively,* lay out the circles of dough in rows on a floured surface. Spoon the filling onto one half of each circle and top with the egg, butter, and olives. Brush the edges with water, fold over as above, and press with the back of a fork to seal the edges. Transfer to the baking sheets.

Bake for 15 to 17 minutes, until lightly browned. Serve immediately.

### Variation: Fried Empanadas

Fill a *caldero* or Dutch oven halfway (no more, or it may spatter or flare up later) with oil or lard and heat over medium-high heat. When a bit of test dough added to the pot is surrounded by a gentle stream of bubbles and you can hear it gently frying, the oil is ready (it should be about 375°F). If it is too cold, the empanadas will be greasy; if is too hot, the crust will blister and be golden before the filling has warmed through. Don't overcrowd the pot. Add the empanadas to the hot oil a few at a time and fry for 5 to 6 minutes, or until golden brown and crisp. Use a splatter screen, and be sure to let the oil return to frying temperature between batches. Transfer to paper towels to drain, and serve hot.

# Empanadas Salteñas

#### FOR THE FILLING

**2 medium boiling potatoes, peeled and cut into**
    **½-inch cubes**
**1 pound well-marbled stewing beef,**
    **such as sirloin tip or triangle (tri-tip)**
**Coarse salt and freshly ground black pepper**
**1 tablespoon unsalted butter**
**½ cup high-quality lard, melted, or**
    **extra virgin olive oil**
**2 medium onions, quartered and very thinly sliced**
**8 scallions, thinly sliced, white and green parts**
    **kept separate**

**1 tablespoon crushed red pepper flakes**
**½ teaspoon ground cumin**
**2 hard-boiled large eggs, coarsely chopped**

**Empanada Dough (recipe follows)**

Put the potato cubes in a saucepan of cold salted water and bring to a boil, then reduce the heat to medium and cook for about 7 minutes, until tender. Drain, wrap in a wet towel so they don't dry out, and set aside.

Trim and discard any gristle from the meat, but leave the fat. With a sharp knife, chop the meat into ⅛-inch pieces. Transfer to a bowl and season with salt and pepper.

Melt the butter with 1 tablespoon of the lard in a large skillet over medium-low heat. Add the onions and stir well, then add the white part of the scallions, and cook until the onions are translucent, about 7 minutes; do not brown. Remove from the heat and set aside.

Heat 2 tablespoons of the lard in a large skillet over high heat. Sear the chopped meat in batches, and spread it out on a tray when it is done, so that it does not steam. When all the meat is browned, combine in a bowl with the onions and the green part of the scallions. Stir in the red pepper flakes and cumin. Add the potato cubes, the remaining 5 tablespoons melted lard, and the chopped eggs. Season to taste with salt and pepper. Cover with plastic wrap and chill until firm. (The filling can be made up to 1 day ahead, but in that case, don't add the eggs until ready to assemble the empanadas.)

Roll out the dough and assemble as for Empanadas Mendocinas (page 55), and bake or deep-fry the empanadas as directed in that recipe.

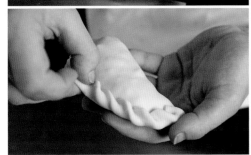

# Empanada Dough

A rolling pin is the traditional tool used for making empanada dough, but if you have a pasta machine, it makes the job easier.

*Salmuera*, water boiled with salt, is a seasoning solution often used in Argentine cookery. The proportions vary from chef to chef and recipe to recipe—for example, the proportion in Chimichurri (page 252) varies from that used here.

**2 cups water**
**1½ tablespoons salt**
**3½ tablespoons high-quality lard, cut into pieces**
**6 to 7 cups all-purpose flour**

For the salmuera, bring the water and salt to a boil in a small saucepan over high heat. Add the lard and stir until it melts, then transfer to a large wide bowl. Allow to cool to room temperature.

Using your hand, gradually add 5½ to 6 cups of the flour, about 1 cup at a time, until you can gather the dough into a ball. Sprinkle ½ cup flour on a work surface to prevent sticking and knead the dough, adding more flour until it will not absorb any more; you want a stiff, dry dough. Divide the dough in half, shape into disks, and wrap in plastic. Chill for at least 1 hour, or up to 24 hours. (The dough can also be frozen, well wrapped, for up to 1 month.)

To finish the assembly of an empanada, I recommend either pinch-pleating or fork-sealing.

# Mussels with Garlic and White Wine

I always make this with sweet tiny mussels like the ones that I collect under the lighthouse of José Ignacio on the beach in Uruguay. Within just a few minutes of starting your fire, you can cook this appetizer on a *chapa*. The billows of white-wine steam and the scent of garlic are dramatic and mouthwatering.

| Serves 4 to 6

**5 pounds mussels, as fresh and small as possible, thoroughly scrubbed and debearded**
**¼ cup extra virgin olive oil**
**8 garlic cloves, minced**
**1 large bunch flat-leaf parsley, minced**
**½ bottle white wine**

Heat a *chapa* or two large cast-iron skillets over high heat until a drop of water sizzles on the surface.

Add the mussels, spread them out evenly, and drizzle the olive oil over them. Scatter the garlic and parsley on top. Scoop the mussels together, using two spatulas, and turn. Pour the white wine over the mussels; this will produce a lot of steam, so be careful. Cover with a large bowl or skillet lids for about 1 minute if the mussels are tiny, or several minutes if they are larger.

The mussels are done once they're open. Discard any unopened mussels, since they are probably bad. Serve immediately.

# Griddled Asparagus with Egg Vinaigrette and Toasted Bread Crumbs

This dish is mainly about texture—nutty, crunchy toasted bread crumbs, smooth egg white bits, and tender, earthy asparagus with a nice char; the red onion adds sharpness and punch. It's a perfect appetizer before a main course of lamb. | Serves 8

**2 pounds thin asparagus**
**¼ cup extra virgin olive oil**
**Coarse salt and freshly ground black pepper**

FOR THE VINAIGRETTE
**½ cup red wine vinegar**
**1 tablespoon Dijon mustard**
**½ cup extra virgin olive oil**
**½ cup minced red onion**
**Whites of 6 hard-boiled eggs, finely chopped**
**½ cup finely chopped fresh flat-leaf parsley**
**Coarse salt and freshly ground black pepper**
**Toasted Fresh Bread Crumbs (page 254)**

Break off the woody ends of the asparagus and discard. Rinse the asparagus and pat dry. Toss with the olive oil and salt and pepper to taste. Set aside.

To make the vinaigrette, whisk the vinegar and the mustard together in a medium bowl. Add the olive oil in a slow, steady stream, whisking constantly until smooth and emulsified. Stir in the onion, chopped egg whites, and parsley. The mixture will be somewhat chunky. Season to taste with salt and pepper.

Heat a *chapa* or large cast-iron skillet over very high heat until it starts to smoke. Add the asparagus in batches and sear for 1 to 2 minutes on each side, until the asparagus is tender and charred in spots but still a bright green color. Transfer to a platter.

To serve, spoon the vinaigrette over the asparagus and top with the bread crumbs.

# Rescoldo Vegetable Plate

Ember-roasting vegetables, the hallmark of the *rescoldo* method (see page 22), is a traditional technique of the Indians of Patagonia. I added pan-melted Cuartirolo cheese. Cuartirolo, originally brought to Argentina by Italian immigrants, is mild and slightly tart. Grilling it gives it a golden crust and a smooth melted interior. | Serves 8

½ cup extra virgin olive oil, plus extra for the pan
2 tablespoons fresh thyme leaves
2 tablespoons fresh oregano leaves
2 teaspoons grated lemon zest
3 Rescoldo Eggplants (page 261)
6 Rescoldo Onions (page 260)
3 Rescoldo Bell Peppers (red, yellow, and/or green; page 260)
2 bunches arugula, trimmed, washed, and dried
6 ounces Cuartirolo cheese (or substitute French Port Salut), sliced ½ inch thick
½ cup chopped Kalamata olives

Pour 6 tablespoons of the olive oil into a small bowl and stir in the thyme, oregano, and lemon zest. Let stand for 1 hour.

Heat a *chapa* or large cast-iron griddle over high heat. Cut the eggplants and onions in half. Brush the cut sides with the remaining 2 tablespoons olive oil and place cut side down on the griddle. Place the peppers on the griddle. Cook for 2 to 3 minutes, without turning, until well browned.

Meanwhile, arrange the arugula on a platter. Top with the vegetables, browned side up.

Wipe off the cooking surface. Brush with a little olive oil, and over medium-high heat brown the cheese on one side only, 1 to 2 minutes. Use a wide spatula to transfer the cheese browned side up to the platter, placing it alongside the vegetables. Drizzle with the herb and lemon oil, sprinkle with the chopped olives, and serve while the cheese is hot.

Photograph on page 63

**ABOVE:** In *rescoldo,* burying vegetables in hot embers and ashes with the
skin left on is a simple technique that produces perfectly cooked vegetables.
**OPPOSITE:** Rescoldo Vegetable Plate (page 61).

# Provoleta

Lightly browned melted provolone cheese seasoned with herbs and hot pepper is a tantalizing combination—salty, spicy, and herbal, with a hint of the barnyard.

Serve with bread while you wait for the meat to come off the *parrilla,* or serve with grilled sausage and a salad for a quick, uncomplicated meal. The traditional recipe calls for dried oregano, but fresh oregano makes for a subtler yet brighter flavor. | Serves 4

**One 1-inch-thick slice provolone (about 8 ounces)**
**3 tablespoons fresh oregano leaves, preferably**
**small ones**
**1 teaspoon crushed red pepper flakes, or to taste**

Heat a *chapa* or cast-iron griddle over low heat until a drop of water sizzles on the surface. Sprinkle the cheese with half the oregano and half the pepper flakes and put on the griddle. Cook for about 2 minutes, until you see the bottom starting to brown and melt, then turn it over with a wide spatula and cook until the second side starts to brown and the cheese is melted. Sprinkle with the remaining oregano and pepper flakes, and serve.

The palmera tree produces a bright orange fruit that we make into a liqueur.

# Charred Calamari Salad

From the sad romantic sound of the *bandoneón* (a type of accordion) in our tango to the pasta on our plates, the traditions brought to Argentina by Italian immigrants have greatly influenced us. Among other dishes, they brought with them their very fresh-tasting seafood salads. This one features tender *calameretti* (baby squid), which are charred until crisp. Avocado, a New World fruit, provides a smooth, creamy contrast.

| Serves 6

4 lemons, halved

4 medium Hass avocados

8 ounces cherry tomatoes, cut in half

2 small red onions, very thinly sliced

1 small bunch flat-leaf parsley,
    leaves removed and minced

½ cup extra virgin olive oil

Coarse salt

1 teaspoon crushed red pepper flakes, or to taste

1 pound cleaned baby calamari, tentacles separated
    from the bodies

Squeeze the juice from the lemons into a large bowl. Split the avocados in half, remove the pits, peel, and cut into ½-inch cubes. Add to the bowl and toss with the lemon juice. Add the cherry tomatoes, red onions, and parsley. Then add ¼ cup of the olive oil, salt to taste, and the crushed red pepper flakes, tossing gently to combine. Set aside.

Rinse the calamari and pat dry. Place in a bowl and toss with the remaining ¼ cup olive oil and salt to taste.

Heat a *chapa* or large cast-iron skillet over high heat until a drop of water sizzles on the surface. Add the calamari in batches, without crowding (if they touch, they will never crisp), and cook on the first side for 2 to 3 minutes, until charred. Turn to the other side and cook for 2 to 3 minutes—no more than 4 or 5 minutes total per batch.

To serve, place the salad in the middle of a deep serving platter and top with the calamari.

Photograph on page 30

# Crisp Sweetbreads with Criolla Salad

Sweetbreads, which are my favorite organ meat, come from the thymus glands of young beef cattle. There are two kinds, those from the throat and those from the pancreas, often referred to as heart sweetbreads. I prefer the "heart" for grilling because it has more fat, which helps develop a deep meaty crust while the insides are creamy and mild, like a flan. Either kind, however, will work for this recipe. If you see any trace of blood, you should soak the sweetbreads in several changes of water, until the water runs clear; if not, you can just rinse them well before you trim them.

The aim here is for crunchy nuggets, so I separate the lobes into large pieces for the preliminary crisping, then divide them into smaller pieces so they can be crisped all around. | Serves 4

1½ pounds sweetbreads, preferably heart
    sweetbreads
6 tablespoons extra virgin olive oil
1 tablespoon coarse salt, or to taste
½ teaspoon freshly ground black pepper, or to taste
4 medium tomatoes, halved and thinly sliced
2 small red onions, halved and thinly sliced
¼ cup Lemon Vinaigrette (page 258)
2 lemons, cut into quarters
4 cups young lettuce leaves, such as Bibb or
    Boston, washed and dried

Wash the sweetbreads under cold running water and pat dry with paper towels. Pull away all the outer membrane, and divide the lobes into 3 or 4 sections along the natural seams. Remove all the exposed membranes, leaving the sweetbreads in large pieces. Rinse them again, pat dry, and put in a medium bowl. Add ¼ cup of the olive oil, the salt, and pepper, turning to coat the sweetbreads.

Combine the tomatoes and onions in a shallow bowl and toss gently with the vinaigrette. Set aside.

Heat a *chapa* or large cast-iron skillet over medium heat until a drop of water sizzles on the surface. Add the sweetbreads and reduce the heat to low. Add 4 lemon quarters to the skillet so that they can brown alongside the sweetbreads; do not squeeze the juice over the sweetbreads—that will prevent them from crisping. Cook the sweetbreads very slowly on the first side until they are nicely caramelized, 10 to 12 minutes. Turn the sweetbreads and lemon quarters, and cook for 6 to 8 more minutes, until well browned on the other side. Transfer the sweetbreads to a cutting board, and discard the lemon wedges.

Separate the sweetbreads into smaller pieces, following the natural seams, as if you were dividing a cauliflower into florets. Raise the heat to medium and coat the hot cast iron with the remaining 2 tablespoons oil. Return the sweetbreads to the hot surface, add the remaining 4 lemon quarters, and adjust the heat. Cook for about 5 minutes, turning occasionally for optimal crunch on all sides, so that the sweetbreads crisp evenly without burning. Turn the lemon quarters as they brown. Drain the sweetbreads briefly on paper towels.

Arrange the lettuce leaves and tomato and onion slices in a serving bowl. Top with the sweetbreads and lemon wedges, toss lightly, and serve immediately.

# Beef

# A Perfect Steak

At the 1992 Seville World's Fair, the Argentine booth was far and away the busiest among the international assortment of food concessions, even though we served only three things: rib-eye steaks, salad, and dulce de leche pancakes. There was a line from the minute we opened until we closed. We served 1,500 steaks a day!

People love a simple steak and salad.

First, the meat. Many cuts of beef can be used for steak—sirloin, porterhouse, shell steak, even costly filet—but as good as they are, they don't achieve perfection. For that, give me a rib eye any time, and make sure it's well-aged and grass-fed beef—only steers raised on grass on the open range produce meat with true depth of flavor, and only a beautifully marbled rib eye has the tenderness and taste that places it at the summit of steaks. Around the outside there is a delicious fatty piece that I call *tapa de bife* ("top of the beefsteak"), and then there's the salty eye: moist and pink on the inside—*bien jugoso* as we say in Spanish, "nice and juicy."

A steak that is seasoned and cooked properly has a salty crust produced by searing. This crust, sublime in its own right, keeps the beef juices from escaping and drying out the meat as the steak cooks. Under that crust, the meat should be basically the same rosy pink throughout. This is your goal, and it can be achieved only if you cook the meat at the proper rate, which is relatively slow in comparison to the sear-and-serve method that produces "black and blue" steaks, which is to say both burnt and raw.

This principle holds true for any beef cooked over direct heat. To get that uniform color, you need even lower heat and longer cooking for thicker cuts.

And now, to the grill.

**One 1-pound boneless rib-eye steak per person,
    about 1¼ to 1½ inches thick**
**Coarse salt**
**Chimichurri (page 252)**

About an hour before you plan to serve the meat, start a wood fire off to the side of the grill. In Argentina, we use a large iron basket for the fire (see photograph, page 13), with a wide grate that allows the larger coals to drop through so you can easily move them under your cooking grill.

Remove the steaks from the fridge or cooler, giving them enough time to come to room temperature. Their temperature will affect the way that heat enters the meat. If it is cold when you put the meat on the grill, you risk toughness.

Shovel or rake a 2- to 3-inch bed of coals under the grill grate. This bed should extend for about 3 inches beyond the perimeter of the grill, so that every part of each steak will receive uniform heat. The grill grate should be 3 to 4 inches from the coals. Wait for the coals to cover over with a layer of whitish ash. You can test the temperature by placing your hand almost at the level that the meat will cook. The fire should be medium-high, and it is ready when you can hold your hand there for only 2½ seconds (to determine 2½ seconds, in Spanish, we say, *"Uno matador, dos matador, tres . . ."*; the English equivalent is "one Mississippi, two Mississippi, three . . ."; see page 13).

Keep a spray bottle filled with water handy to douse any flare-ups.

Salt the steaks to taste. Using tongs, grease the grill grate with a piece of fat or a clean cloth or paper towel moistened with olive oil or other cooking oil.

Place the meat on the grill. You should hear a nice sizzle. Then don't touch the steaks, and don't move them. After 5 minutes, gently lift one edge to check the sear marks on the meat. If they look just right at that point, rotate the meat 90 degrees. This will create a crosshatch pattern and keep the meat from burning where it is in contact with the grill.

After 4 more minutes, turn the steaks over and cook for another 7 minutes, or until cooked to medium-rare. As before, check after 5 minutes to make sure the meat doesn't burn where it touches the grill, and rotate the steaks if necessary.

Transfer the steaks to a platter and let rest for 3 minutes.

Serve with Chimichurri.

That's all it takes for perfection. But, as with many things that are perfect and simple, you will need to develop your own sense of fire, heat, and ingredients. For example, the temperature test recommended above is a good guideline but not an unbreakable rule; your hand may be more or less sensitive to heat than mine. And if you are cooking on a cold day or a windy one, that will affect how long the meat takes to cook. The leanness or fattiness of the meat and the degree of aging also come into play. With time and practice, though, I promise you will be able to gauge your steaks by the sound, touch, and smell of cooking.

If you cook a steak over the proper heat (see recipe), it will have a well-seared crust and be uniform in color and juiciness throughout.

A Sunday Asado

For many families, including my own, the *asado* is often the weekend's main event. It begins with a morning pilgrimage to the butcher shop to choose the impressive quantities and varieties of meat, continues with building the fire and waiting for the coals to be just right, and it reaches critical mass when the food goes on the grill, the wine is poured, and the fire hisses and snaps. Inevitably, because everyone has an opinion, there is

much discussion as to the proper heat, the doneness of the meat, the advisability of turning the meat, and so forth. The reward for being part of such debates is usually a freshly cut slice of crusty, juicy, perfectly sea-soned meat offered by the grillmaster, or *asador*. In the end, he—or she—has the final say.

The beauty and challenge of an *asado* is cooking many different things that will come off the grill at dif-ferent times. It's the duty of the *asador* to keep serv-ing delicious meat nonstop until there are just some bones left for the dog. But you'll never enjoy prepar-ing an *asado* if you're a slave to cooking times. True, it requires attention, but over time, you'll develop a sixth sense about what's happening on the grill and what needs to be done next. Don't be intimidated by the scale of it all. Grilling is an art, but a forgiving one. North Americans should know that it's okay to test for doneness by cutting off a piece now and then.

### MENU FOR 12
**Pears with Ibérico Ham, Parsley, Olive Oil,
   and Garlic Sauce (page 34)**
**Provoleta (page 64)**
**Crusty baguettes**
**Sausages**
***Tira de asado* (short ribs)**
**Chimichurri (page 252)**
**Beef tri-tip**
**Ember-roasted potatoes, sweet potatoes,
   peppers, and onions**
**Sweetbreads**
**Whole rib eye on the bone**
**Fresh seasonal fruit**

### SHOPPING LIST
**1 whole standing rib roast, about 9½ pounds**
**1½ to 2 pounds sirloin tri-tip roast**
**3 pounds short ribs, cut crosswise into strips about
   ¾ inch thick (about 8 ounces each)**
**3 pounds fresh sausages (any combination
   of Italian sweet or hot sausage, fresh chorizo,
   and/or fresh morcilla)**
**2 pounds sweetbreads**
**1½ pounds provolone, cut into 3 thick slices**
**8 potatoes**
**8 sweet potatoes**
**10 onions**
**6 large bell peppers—red, green, or yellow or
   a combination**
**Extra virgin olive oil**
**Coarse salt**
**6 baguettes**

» To begin serving at 2:00, start your fire at 11:00 a.m. You will need at least 15 to 20 logs for this menu. Have another half dozen on hand just in case. Charcoal will also work, in which case plan on two 10-pound bags with an extra in reserve.

## SATURDAY

» Shop for ingredients (you may have to preorder special cuts from your butcher), including fresh seasonal fruit for dessert (you're not going to have room to eat anything more than that).

» Make 8 cups Chimichurri and 4 cups Salmuera (page 252).

» Choose the wines. Rustic and red is never wrong.

» Set up the grill area; assemble the wood or charcoal and tools: shovel, coal rake, and a fireplace poker or tongs for moving burning wood.

» Gather all the other equipment: large wooden carving board, assorted knives, a carving set (knife and large fork), long kitchen tongs, fireproof oven mitts, spray bottle of water to tamp down flare-ups, instant-read thermometer, timer, paper towels, serving platters, cutting boards.

## SUNDAY

### 9 to 10 a.m.

» Unwrap large cuts of meats, arrange on a large tray, cover loosely with butcher paper, and bring to room temperature. (If it is a hot day, wait an extra hour before taking the large cuts from the refrigerator.)

» Thoroughly rinse the sweetbreads in cold water for a few minutes, and return to the refrigerator. Keep cold until 11 a.m.

» Prepare the pears and garlic sauce. Cover and set aside or refrigerate.

### 11 a.m.

» Start your fire. For a typical *asado,* figure on a grate about 24 by 36 inches; this includes space for the vegetables. Think about where you will place your items, leaving plenty of room around each cut of meat. If you crowd them, they will steam rather than developing a gorgeous crust.

» Remove the rest of the meats from the refrigerator. Bring the cheese to room temperature.

» Set up a table with all the cooking equipment.

» Set up the serving area with plates, cutlery, napkins, and glasses; tubs of ice for cold drinks, water or soft drinks, and wines, and a corkscrew; a bread knife and basket; assorted serving platters; and small bowls of coarse salt, crushed red pepper flakes, and oregano, and a peppermill. Have a wide spatula and griddle ready for the Provoleta (page 64).

» Slice the cheese for the Provoleta, and sprinkle with the herbs.

## 12 noon

» Distribute coals under the grill, allowing for areas of varying heat intensity.

» Rib roast (total cooking time 2 to 2½ hours): Pat dry with paper towels and season with salt. Oil the grill grate. Put the rib roast bone side down over a medium-hot area (set the timer for 45 minutes).

» Sweetbreads (2 hours): Oil the grate in a low-heat area and put the sweetbreads on the grill.

## 12:30 p.m.

» Uncork the wine. Slice the baguettes.

» Check the sweetbreads and rib roast.

## 12:45 p.m.

» Turn the rib roast (set timer for 45 minutes again).

## 1 p.m.

» Guests arrive—your busiest hour.

» Guests can serve themselves at the bar.

» Serve the pears.

» Put the potatoes, sweet potatoes, onions, and peppers in the coals (see Rescoldo Vegetable Plate, page 61).

## 1:15 p.m.

» Heat a griddle and melt the Provoleta. Transfer the melted cheese to a platter and let guests serve themselves, with bread.

## 1:30 p.m.

» Turn the rib roast and sweetbreads.

» Pat the tri-tip dry with paper towels. Season with salt and put over medium-high heat. Brown well, turning occasionally; this will take at least 15 minutes.

» Turn the vegetables.

» Pat the short ribs dry. Season with salt, place over medium-high heat, and brown well on the first side, about 12 minutes.

## 1:40 to 1:45 p.m.

» Turn the tri-tip and short ribs. Check the vegetables and turn as needed.

» Put the sausages over medium heat; turn after approximately 10 minutes.

» Keep checking the rib roast, turning it and cooking until a crunchy crust forms on all sides; if necessary, stand it on end. Finish it bone side down. When grilling large bone-in cuts of meat, most of the cooking should be done with the bone side toward the fire: the bones conduct heat, so that it enters the interior of the meat and cooks it in a gentle and uniform way.

## 2:00 p.m.

» The short ribs are ready when they are browned on both sides and red juices pool on top. Transfer to a carving board and carve into riblets. Serve with chimichurri.

» The tri-tip should be almost ready. Turn to make sure that it is caramelized on all sides, and slice off a piece to test for doneness. When it is ready, remove from the fire and rest for 10 minutes.

» Serve the sweetbreads, sausages, and vegetables as they are ready. The sweetbreads should be crisp-tender and cooked through. The sausages should be juicy but completely cooked, and the vegetables charred and tender.

» Meanwhile, check on the rib roast. When an instant-read thermometer inserted into the center reads 125°F, take it off the fire and let it rest for 15 minutes before carving. Carve the meat off the bone in one piece, and throw the bones back on the fire to crisp on both sides. (If you want your meat more well done, put it back on the fire for 5 to 10 minutes.) Slice the meat. Cut the bones apart and serve with the meat.

» For dessert, serve the fresh fruit.

The Andes, stretching from the northern end of Argentina all the way to the southernmost parts of Patagonia, are our "west coast."

# Churrasco

When an Argentine is in the mood for a quick and easy steak, the first thing that comes to mind is a *churrasco*. The exact cut for a *churrasco* may vary from place to place but for me it means flavorful, chewy rump steak. It is hard to find ones that I like in the United States, so I've substituted shell steak here. | Serves 4

**Four ½-inch-thick shell steaks, about 8 ounces each**
**2 tablespoons extra virgin olive oil**
**Coarse salt**
**Chimichurri (page 252)**

Heat a *chapa* or one or two large cast-iron skillets over high heat. Brush the steaks with the olive oil and sprinkle with coarse salt. When the surface is very hot, add the steaks and sear them, without moving them, for at least 1½ minutes or until well browned—lift up an edge of one steak with tongs to check. Turn the steaks and cook for another minute, or until done to taste. Transfer to a platter and let rest for 1 minute.

Serve with the chimichurri.

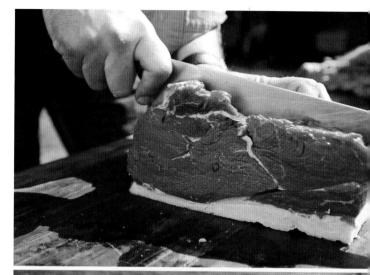

# Bricklayer Steak

Around eleven o'clock in the morning, the construction workers at nearly every work site in Buenos Aires pause for lunch. They don't have time to wait for a fire to burn down to a bed of coals, so they build a quick fire with scrap wood. Once the fire gets going, they put a *chapa* over it and grill a thin steak. In honor of the bricklayers, carpenters, and all the building trades of the city, here's the version we serve at Patagonia Sur in La Boca.

Serve with Charred Sweet Potato Strips (page 260).

| Serves 4

**2 pounds butterflied beef tenderloin, pounded to ½ inch or slightly thinner (you can ask your butcher to do this for you; see Note)**

FOR THE MARINADE

**4 bay leaves**
**1 tablespoon crushed red pepper flakes**
**1 tablespoon *pimentón dulce* (sweet Spanish smoked paprika)**
**1 head garlic, separated into cloves, smashed, and peeled**
**1 small bunch oregano**
**1 teaspoon black peppercorns**
**½ cup extra virgin olive oil**

FOR THE GUACAMOLE

**1 small red onion, finely chopped**
**1 small red bell pepper, finely chopped**
**4 small Hass avocados**
**Juice of 2 lemons**
**1 small bunch cilantro or flat-leaf parsley, leaves removed and finely chopped**
**1 jalapeño chile, finely chopped**
**2 tablespoons extra virgin olive oil**
**Coarse salt and freshly ground black pepper**

FOR THE TOMATO SALAD

**4 small ripe tomatoes, sliced**
**4 scallions, sliced**
**1 tablespoon red wine vinegar**
**2 tablespoons extra virgin olive oil**
**¼ cup finely chopped fresh flat-leaf parsley**
**Coarse salt and freshly ground black pepper**

**¼ cup crème fraîche**

To marinate the beef, cut the meat into 4 equal pieces. Place in a baking dish and add the bay leaves. Combine the red pepper flakes, *pimentón,* garlic cloves, oregano, peppercorns, and olive oil in a small bowl and pour over the meat, turning to coat all sides. Refrigerate for at least 8 hours or overnight.

To make the guacamole, combine the onion and red bell pepper in a bowl. Halve, pit, and peel the avocados. Chop into tiny dice, add to the onion and bell pepper, and toss with the lemon juice. Stir in the cilantro or parsley, jalapeño, and olive oil. Season with salt and pepper to taste. Set aside.

To make the salad, combine the tomatoes, scallions, vinegar, olive oil, and parsley in a small bowl. Season with salt and pepper to taste. Set aside.

Heat a *chapa* or one or two cast-iron skillets over medium-high heat until a drop of water sizzles on the surface. Place the meat on the hot surface (don't brush off the herbs and spices) and cook, without moving, for about 3 minutes on the first side, 2 minutes on the other, or until medium rare.

To serve, spread each steak with 1 tablespoon crème fraîche. Top with a large spoonful of guacamole. Serve with the tomato salad on the side.

NOTE: Corn-fed beef lacks the necessary texture for this dish; grass-fed is the only way to go.

# Tournedos Wrapped in Bacon and Sage

I haven't been able to take this dish off my menu since I served it at age nineteen in my first restaurant, in Bariloche. That place was called Nahuel Malal, "The Pelt of the Mountain Lion," in honor of our rare Andean pumas. Some years ago, near my mountain cabin in Patagonia, my children Alexia and Francisco and I saw a pair of them at first light. Each night for the rest of our stay, we left food for them, and each morning it was gone. | Serves 4

**4 strips slab bacon, cut ⅛ inch thick and about an
  inch wide, or 4 strips lightly smoked bacon**
**4 beef tournedos, cut 1 inch thick, about 5 ounces
  each (see Note)**
**16 fresh sage leaves**
**Coarse salt and freshly ground black pepper**

Place the bacon in a saucepan with 4 cups cold water, bring to a simmer, and blanch for 5 minutes. Drain and pat dry with paper towels.

Pat the tournedos dry. Wrap a strip of bacon around the circumference of each, evenly spacing 4 sage leaves in each bundle. Tie with kitchen string.

Heat a *chapa* or large cast-iron skillet over high heat until it starts to smoke and a drop of water sizzles on the surface. Sprinkle the tournedos with salt and pepper and stand them on their sides on the hot surface, so that the bacon is in contact with the hot pan. Cook, without moving them, for 1½ to 2 minutes, until the bacon is well charred. Rotate the tournedos a quarter turn and cook until the bacon is crisped, then repeat two more times so the bacon is nicely crisped all around. Turn the tournedos to their flat sides and cook for 2 to 3 minutes on each side for medium-rare. Transfer to a platter and let rest for 3 minutes.

Remove the string, and serve the steak.

NOTE: Tournedos are steaks cut from the tenderloin, also known as filet mignon.

# A La Vara

*A la vara* is a favored cooking method among our native peoples in the northeast. What I like most about it is that all you need to cook *a la vara* on a hike or camping trip are the ingredients, a knife, and a match—no pots, no pans.

Here, as elsewhere, the trick to success is to keep the ingredients from coming into direct contact with the flames. Intense heat is good, but burning isn't, so watch the fire constantly. There is no real indoor equivalent for this cooking method, but I imagine one could do it the same way Charles Lamb did in his satirical "Dissertation upon Roast Pig," where you place a pig in a house and then burn the house down!

**DEFINITION:** This is perhaps the most low-tech grilling method I know. Two sharpened Y-shaped branches are inserted in the ground to hold a spit fashioned from a green branch, itself sharpened on one end. The meat is threaded on the spit.

**TEMPERATURE CONTROL:** To adjust heat, move the stakes toward or away from the fire—toward if you want more heat, and away if you want less. You can also place coals or embers directly under your skewer.

**ABOVE:** Its bark removed and its end sharpened, a green branch serves as a skewer or spit. **OPPOSITE:** I'm cooking *a la vara* here as a sideshow to a big *caldero* fire, but on its own an *a la vara* fire can be quite small.

# Skirt Steak and Fry Bread

## Entraña a la Vara

When cooked properly, skirt steak is quite tender and juicy, or *bien jugoso,* which is the highest compliment an Argentine or Uruguayan can pay to any grill master. I always shop for *entraña* with a healthy dose of skepticism—since the part of the cow that it comes from sits right on top of the guts, it has to be very fresh. When the steak is cooked *a la vara* and served with fry bread, you don't even need a fork to pick up the slices of meat. | Serves 4

**1 skirt steak, about 2 pounds**
**Coarse salt and freshly ground black pepper**
**Fry Bread (page 247)**

About 45 minutes before you're ready to cook, use 5 whole rounds and 5 split rounds to build a fire, downwind of your dining area or campsite.

Meanwhile, prepare your stakes and skewer: For the stakes, use two Y-shaped branches (preferably green) about 24 inches in length. If necessary, using a knife or hatchet, carefully sharpen the stakes to a point so that they can be pushed into the ground easily.

Push the stakes about 6 inches deep into the ground, about 18 inches to 2 feet to the side of the fire, so that the meat will receive even, medium-high heat.

For the skewer, use a knife to peel the bark from another green branch and sharpen it so that it can pierce the steak.

Season the meat with salt and pepper and thread it onto the skewer as shown in the photographs on pages 85 and 86.

If necessary, rearrange the fire so that the whole steak continues to receive even heat. Place the skewer on the stakes.

Cook for about 6 minutes on the first side, and then about 3 minutes on the other. If your fire is hot enough, the meat will be seared and caramelized after 6 minutes. If the fire is not hot enough, you may adjust the heat by leaning the stakes toward the fire.

Cut the steak into ½-inch-thick slices against the grain, and serve with the fry bread.

# Braided Beef with Anchovies and Olives

I created this recipe for a restaurant I helped launch in São Paulo, Brazil. Serving meat, meat, and more meat to six hundred customers a day can get the chef in a rut. I was looking for some variety on the menu. This braided fillet is the result.

You need to have a good relationship with your butcher for this—or become one yourself. It is essential to use a solid center-cut piece of beef fillet, partially butterflied so that you can cut it into three long strips still attached at one end. This is expensive, and many butchers don't like to give you this cut, because then they're stuck with the ends. If that's the case, you can buy a whole fillet and trim it yourself; cut the rest into tournedos or meat for kebabs and freeze. | Serves 2

15 anchovy fillets, rinsed and patted dry

1 cup pitted Kalamata olives

1 center-cut beef tenderloin roast,
    at least 12 inches long, partially butterflied

2 tablespoons extra virgin olive oil

Freshly ground black pepper

Crush the anchovies to a paste in a mortar (or pulse in a food processor). Chop half the olives, and crush them together with the anchovies. Cut the fillet lengthwise into 3 long strips, stopping 1 inch from the end. Spread the anchovy mixture evenly along one side of each strip. Braid the meat tightly, tying it firmly together at the end with kitchen string (see photographs opposite). Use your palms to flatten the braid to an even thickness, then push any anchovy stuffing back into the braids. Brush the meat all over with 1 tablespoon of the olive oil.

Brush a *chapa* or large cast-iron griddle with the remaining 1 tablespoon olive oil and heat over medium heat until a drop of water sizzles on the surface. Add the beef and cook for 10 minutes, without moving it, or until it is nicely browned on the first side. Turn the meat over and sear on the other side for about 6 minutes—the meat should still be quite rare. Continue turning and cooking the meat until all sides are seared and it is done to taste. Transfer the meat to a carving board and let it rest for 5 minutes.

Meanwhile, lightly smash the remaining olives and place alongside the meat. The juices will run together.

Remove the string, carve the beef into thick slices, and season with pepper. Serve with the olives and juices.

Photograph on page 93

ABOVE: Whenever I build a new home or restaurant, one of the first additions is a family-sized table under a shady tree. OPPOSITE: Braided Beef with Anchovies and Olives (page 90).

# Beef and Potato Pie

This recipe probably came to Argentina with Welsh immigrants in the nineteenth century. To this day, you'll find many of their redheaded descendants with the surname Jones in the Patagonian state of Chubut.

It looks like the familiar shepherd's pie that is a British pub standard, but don't be fooled. Inside there's an earthy, complex, smoky mingling of warm spices—cumin and *pimentón,* dry mustard, a bit of chile pepper—Kalamata olives, and tomatoes, all melded together with the local red wine. | Serves 6 to 8

1 tablespoon extra virgin olive oil

2 onions, chopped

2 carrots, peeled and chopped

2 pounds ground sirloin

2 bay leaves

2 teaspoons chopped fresh rosemary leaves

2 teaspoons chopped fresh oregano leaves

1½ teaspoons ground cumin

1½ teaspoons *pimentón dulce*
    (sweet Spanish smoked paprika)

1 teaspoon crushed red pepper flakes

1 tablespoon dry mustard

1 cup dry red wine

1 pound ripe tomatoes, thinly sliced

1 cup pitted Kalamata olives

Coarse salt and freshly ground black pepper

4 large Idaho (baking) potatoes, peeled and
    cut into 2-inch chunks

1 cup whole milk

6 large egg yolks

2 hard-boiled eggs

1½ teaspoons sugar (optional)

Combine the olive oil, onions, and carrots in a large cast-iron skillet and sauté over medium-high heat, stirring, for about 5 minutes, until the vegetables soften and begin to brown. Crumble in the ground sirloin and cook for about 4 minutes, breaking up the meat with a fork, until it loses its pink color. Stir in the bay leaves, rosemary, oregano, cumin, *pimentón,* pepper flakes, and mustard. Add the red wine and let it bubble gently for 5 minutes to evaporate the alcohol.

Stir in the tomatoes and olives and season to taste with salt and pepper. Reduce the heat to low and simmer for 20 minutes, or until the meat is very tender and the liquid is reduced but not totally evaporated. (It is important that the finished dish be moist.) Remove from the heat.

Meanwhile, put the potatoes in a medium pot with cold water to cover, add salt to taste, and bring to a boil over high heat. Reduce the heat slightly and boil for about 15 minutes, until the potatoes are very tender when pierced with a fork. Drain the potatoes thoroughly in a colander, and pass through a food mill or a ricer back into the pot.

Bring the milk to a boil, and beat it into the potatoes with a wooden spoon. One by one, beat in the egg yolks, and continue beating until well blended, fluffy, and yellow.

Heat an *horno* or home oven (with the rack positioned in the lower third of the oven) to approximately 375°F.

Slice the hard-boiled eggs ⅓ inch thick and arrange them over the meat mixture. Spoon the mashed potatoes on top and smooth the surface with a spatula. Use the tines of a fork to press a pattern of fine decorative ridges over the entire surface of the potatoes. Sprinkle with the sugar, if using.

Bake for 30 to 35 minutes, until the potatoes are nicely browned on top.

# Veal Chops with Fresh Bread Crumbs

The secret to the succulence of these veal chops is fresh bread crumbs and clarified butter in a breading that is slowly fried. The result is both crisp and juicy. I'm writing this while having one of these chops for lunch. Actually, one and a half: my daughters Ambar and Alegra ordered one to share, but they lost interest when our dog, Luna, wanted to play, so I am also finishing theirs. That's a lot of meat, even for an Argentine. | Serves 2

2 veal rib chops, about 1 pound each
3 cups soft bread crumbs
3 large eggs
1 tablespoon minced garlic
3 tablespoons chopped fresh flat-leaf parsley
1 teaspoon coarse salt
Freshly ground black pepper
2 to 4 tablespoons Clarified Butter (page 255)
2 cups arugula leaves
1 cup radicchio leaves torn into bite-sized pieces
1 ripe tomato, diced
Lemon wedges (optional)

Lay the veal chops on a work surface. Do not trim the excess fat yet. With a meat pounder, pound the meat extending from the bone to an even thickness of ½ inch. Now trim the excess fat.

Spread the bread crumbs on a tray. Lightly beat the eggs with the minced garlic, parsley, salt, and pepper to taste in a wide bowl. Soak the veal in the egg mixture, turning to thoroughly drench both sides, then transfer the veal to the bread crumbs and turn to coat both sides. Wipe the crumbs off the ends of the bones.

If you want to brown the veal bones before serving (see below), preheat the oven to 400°F.

Heat 2 tablespoons of the clarified butter on a *chapa* or in a square or rectangular cast-iron griddle over low heat. Add the veal chops and cook very slowly until the bread crumbs are golden, about 10 minutes; your goal is to crisp the breading without drying it out, so it is important that the heat be just high enough to make a slight sizzling sound. If the breading becomes dry, add half-tablespoons of butter around the veal as it cooks, lifting the chops to let the butter flow under the meat. Turn and cook on the other side in the same manner for about 10 minutes more, until the veal is cooked to medium and the crumbs are crisp and golden.

If desired, transfer the griddle to the oven to brown the bones—no longer than 5 minutes. It is purely for cosmetic reasons that you lightly brown the bones; take care not to dry out the bread crumbs. Meanwhile, combine the arugula and radicchio.

Lightly blot the veal chops with a paper towel to absorb any extra butter. Transfer to dinner plates and cover with the salad, then spoon the diced tomatoes over the top. Serve with lemon wedges, if desired.

# Carbonada in a Pumpkin

Argentina's Independence Day is July 9, which is deepest winter in the Southern Hemisphere. When I was growing up in Bariloche, we marked it with a great carnival, and I adored the festivities—all kinds of wonderful games with prizes. In the same way that Americans on the Fourth of July have hamburgers, hot dogs, spareribs, and fried chicken, we have our *carbonada*.

| Serves 4

1 Andean-type pumpkin (or zapallo) or ambercup
    squash, about 4 pounds
Coarse salt
1 tablespoon unsalted butter
4 bay leaves
3 fresh thyme sprigs
6 garlic cloves, smashed and peeled
6 black peppercorns
½ cup milk or broth (beef, chicken, or vegetable)
⅔ cup canned plum tomatoes, with their juice
1⅔ cups beef stock
2 tablespoons extra virgin olive oil
4 ounces pancetta (ask the butcher to slice the
    pancetta ⅓ inch thick), cut into ⅓-inch dice
1 fresh rosemary sprig
1 pound tender stewing beef, cut into ½-inch pieces
Freshly ground black pepper
1 tablespoon red wine vinegar
2 small onions, finely chopped
⅛ teaspoon sugar
2 carrots, peeled and cut into ½-inch dice
1 cup dry red wine
1 large red potato, peeled and cut into ½-inch dice
1 sweet potato, peeled and cut into ½-inch dice
1 ear corn, husked and cut into 6 pieces
2 ripe peaches, pitted and quartered

Heat an *horno* or home oven (with the rack positioned in the lower third of the oven) to approximately 375°F.

Slice the top 2 inches off the pumpkin, leaving the stem intact. With a large sharp spoon, scrape away all the fibers and seeds from both sections. Prick the inside of the pumpkin all over with a fork. Sprinkle generously with salt. Stand the bottom part of the pumpkin in a roasting pan and put the butter, 2 of the bay leaves, the thyme sprigs, 2 of the garlic cloves, and the peppercorns into the cavity. Pour in the milk or broth and cover with the top of the pumpkin.

Bake for 1 hour, or until the pumpkin is tender when pierced through the side with a bamboo skewer. If it starts to brown before it is tender, cover loosely with foil.

Meanwhile, combine the canned tomatoes and beef stock in a saucepan and bring to a simmer over medium heat, crushing the tomatoes with a wooden spoon. Simmer for 5 minutes to blend the flavors. Remove from the heat and set aside.

Heat the olive oil in a *caldero* or large Dutch oven over medium-high heat. Add the diced pancetta, the remaining 2 bay leaves, and the rosemary sprig and sauté until the pancetta becomes translucent and renders its fat. Add the beef and the remaining 4 garlic cloves, raise the heat to high, and cook until the meat is well browned on all sides. Season with salt and pepper, add the red wine vinegar, and boil until the liquid has evaporated. Add the onions and stir in the sugar. Remove the rosemary and add the carrots, then pour in the red wine, bring to a boil, and let it bubble for about 5 minutes, until the alcohol has cooked off. Add the potato, sweet potato, and tomato-stock mixture and bring to a boil. Lower the heat to a simmer, add the corn and the

peaches, partially cover the pot, and simmer until the meat and vegetables are tender, about 15 minutes. Remove the bay leaves, adjust the seasoning, and keep warm.

To serve, empty out the pumpkin. Set it upright on a large deep serving platter. Spoon the stew into the pumpkin, set the lid on top, and take to the table. Using a large sharp serving spoon, spoon the *carbonada* onto individual soup plates, scooping out some pumpkin flesh with each serving.

# Whole Boneless Rib Eye with Chimichurri

I usually cook roasts on the bone because I like the way bones gently conduct heat into the meat. But when you slather a coating of chimichurri on a boneless rib roast, the result is the most heavenly crust you can imagine. Just keep an eye on the cooking time and the internal temperature. Since all ovens vary, the timings given below are just guidelines that you may need to adjust in your own oven. | Serves 20

**1 boneless rib-eye roast, 6 to 10 pounds**
**Coarse salt**
**2 cups Chimichurri (page 252), or more if desired**
**6 bay leaves**

Heat an *horno* or home oven (with the rack positioned in the lower third of the oven) to approximately 450°F.

Pat the meat dry with paper towels. Sprinkle with coarse salt and coat on all sides with half the chimichurri (reserve the rest for serving). Scatter the bay leaves over the meat. Place on a rack in a large roasting pan and roast for 20 minutes. Lower the heat to 350°F and roast for approximately 10 minutes more per pound for rare (120°F). Transfer to a carving board and let rest for at least 10 minutes.

Carve the beef and serve with the remaining chimichurri.

Una Vaca Entera

A cross between a banquet and a construction project, this is without question the most ambitious—though not the most complicated—recipe in the book. Out on the pampas, gauchos will sometimes cook a whole cow *(una vaca entera)*, hide and all. I first saw this done in the early 1970s on an *estancia* called La Peregrina, in the cattle country outside Buenos Aires.

After I'd done this myself a few times, CNN heard about it and asked whether they could film it. It was the dead of winter when we planned to cook in a chestnut grove in the mountains outside Mendoza. I brought one of my chefs, Hugo, from Buenos Aires. We dropped off the cow (and some lambs for the evening meal) and then the crew and I returned to Mendoza for more supplies, leaving Hugo to light the cooking fires at dusk. We were delayed in town and didn't get back to the chestnut grove until midnight. Meanwhile, Hugo, being a city boy, wasn't accustomed to the mountains and wildlife, so when a group of foxes began to gather—attracted no doubt by the smell of so much meat cooking—he climbed a tree. When we finally returned, there was poor Hugo freezing in the tree, vowing never to return to the countryside. His mood improved once we drank some wine. We ate, played guitars, and tended the fire through the night.

I've since cooked a whole cow a few times, most recently for Anthony Bourdain's television show, *No Reservations*. I had never met Bourdain before, but we instantly connected as two chefs who like our food done as simply as possible—the more primitive the better.

So on the chance that you have a cow or two that you'd like to cook, here is the recipe. I must confess, after a lifetime of following fancy French recipes, that it gives me great pleasure to write the following list of ingredients:

**1 medium cow, about 1400 pounds, butterflied, skin removed**

**2 gallons Salmuera (2 cup salt, 8 quarts water, boiled to dissolve; see headnote, page 57)**

**2 gallons Chimichurri (page 252)**

EQUIPMENT AND OTHER SUPPLIES

**1 heavy-duty block-and-tackle attached to a steel stanchion set in concrete**

**1 two-sided truss made of heavy-duty steel**

**One 9-foot-square sheet of corrugated metal**

**1 pair of heavy-duty pliers**

**2 cords hardwood logs**

## THE DAY BEFORE

### 7 p.m.

» Start the fire, using about 20 large logs.

### 8 p.m.

» With the aid of eight strong helpers, put the cow in the truss. Sprinkle with salmuera and raise to a 45-degree angle, with the bone side facing the fire. Place the sheet of corrugated metal over the skin side to reflect and contain the heat (as you would tent a turkey). Arrange the coals under the cow so that the whole cow receives even, slow heat.

### 10 p.m.

» Sprinkle the meat again with salmuera. Continue to add logs to the bonfire and coals to the cooking fire all through the night. Take turns napping, with one member of the crew tending the fire. You might also roast a lamb *al asador* (see page 112) to feed your crew through the night.

## THE DAY OF YOUR FEAST

### 10 a.m.

» Remove the corrugated reflector. Brush the cow with salmuera. Turn the cow and brush that side with salmuera too. Continue to cook, crisping the meat.

### 2 p.m.

» Begin to carve (some parts may require longer cooking), and serve with the chimichurri.

Roasting a cow is definitely a "team sport." From left: arranging the cow on the truss; adding coals to keep a good uniform cooking temperature; and seasoning with salmuera for a delicious salty crust.

# Lamb, Pork, & Chicken

Lamb al Asador

My grade-school principal, Edith Jones—a descendant of the first Welsh immigrants—prepared the first lamb *al asador* I can remember. If I close my eyes when I smell the cooking aromas of roast lamb, I'm transported back to her farm outside Bariloche, where she often invited our family on Sunday afternoons. I see myself standing beside a lamb on a cross that appeared to be bigger than me. I was hypnotized by it, watching the juices drip, hearing the fat puff as it hit the ashes.

MENU FOR 12 TO 15

**1 whole baby lamb (about 25 pounds), butterflied**

**4 cups salmuera (4 cups water, ¼ cup salt, boiled to dissolve; see headnote, page 57)**

**8 to 12 Idaho (baking) potatoes**

**8 to 12 onions, unpeeled**

**8 to 12 bell peppers—a combination of red, green, and yellow**

**Other vegetables (butternut or acorn squash, eggplant, etc., as desired)**

**Chimichurri (page 252)**

**Salsa Criolla (page 253)**

» To serve the lamb for lunch at 2:00, start your fire with kindling and about 10 logs approximately 6 inches in diameter at 6 a.m. Have another 15 logs ready to feed the fire during cooking. (If using charcoal, start a 10-pound bag at 7:00 a.m. and have another 10-pound bag in reserve to feed the fire.)

### 7:30 a.m.

» Truss the lamb, attaching it to the iron cross. Sprinkle the bone side with salmuera, and set the *asador* in the ground, with the bone side facing the fire, 6 to 9 feet away for medium-low heat.

### 8:00 a.m.

» Start the cooking, adjusting the heat as necessary by leaning the cross toward or away from the flame.

### 12:00 noon

» If the lamb came with the kidneys still attached, remove and serve them.

### 12:30 p.m.

» Sprinkle the outside of the lamb with more salmuera and turn it so that the bone side is away from the fire. Sprinkle the bone side with the remaining salmuera. You may need to rake some coals from the fire to just under the lamb to make sure that the skin side crisps and cooks evenly; make deeper mounds of coals under the parts that need more heat.

### 1:00 p.m.

» Nestle the vegetables in the embers, covering them as much as possible with hot ashes.

### 2:00 p.m.

» Test the lamb for doneness by cutting off a slice; the outside should be nice and crispy. When the internal temperature is approximately 140°F, transfer the lamb to a table or other work surface and let it rest for 10 to 20 minutes.

» Meanwhile, remove the vegetables from the embers and brush away the ashes.

» Carve the lamb and serve with the chimichurri, salsa criolla, and vegetables.

# 7½-Hour Lamb Malbec
# with Rosemary and Lemon

This is one of my signature dishes, developed years ago with my longtime sous chef, German Martinegui, who is now one of the top chefs in Buenos Aires. At that time, the fashionable French chefs were slow-cooking many things for 7 hours—it was kind of shorthand for old-fashioned, deep-flavored braises and stews. Since Patagonian lamb is all grass-fed, our animals run and get exercise and, as a result, the meat can stand up to longer cooking. (We chose 7½ hours for the name because we liked the movie 9½ *Weeks*.) Lamb has a strong taste and it takes a powerful wine such as Malbec to complement it. If you find that the meat is beginning to fall apart after 3 or 4 hours (American lamb may take less time to become tender), take it off the flame and let it steep in its juices until it has been in the pot for the full amount of time.

This dish is best if you cook it a day or even two days ahead. Also, if you refrigerate the cooked lamb, it is easier to cut neatly into serving portions (hot meat tends to shred). Serve with mashed potatoes or creamy polenta to soak up the rich sauce. | Serves 8

1 boneless leg of lamb, 5 to 6 pounds
   (see headnote)
Coarse salt and freshly ground black pepper
⅓ cup fresh rosemary leaves, minced
2 cups fresh flat-leaf parsley leaves, minced
¼ cup Lemon Confit (page 259), minced
8 garlic cloves, minced, plus 1 head garlic, skin on,
   cut horizontally in half
½ cup olive oil
3 carrots, peeled and cut into 4 pieces each
3 leeks, trimmed, quartered lengthwise, and
   thoroughly rinsed
2 onions, quartered
2 celery stalks, cut into 4 pieces each
2 small fennel bulbs, trimmed and quartered

2 teaspoons black peppercorns
2 bay leaves
2 bottles (750 ml) Malbec

If the lamb is not already tied, carefully trim any gristle and most of the fat from the meat. Open it out flat and sprinkle with coarse salt and pepper.

Combine the minced rosemary, parsley, lemon confit, and minced garlic in a small bowl, add ¼ cup of the olive oil, and mix thoroughly. Spread evenly over the surface of the lamb. Roll it up and tie it with butcher's string. If the lamb is already rolled and tied, use your fingers to push the herb and lemon mixture as deeply as possible into all of the seams. Pat the lamb dry, and season with salt and pepper.

Heat 2 tablespoons olive oil in a large cast-iron skillet over medium-high heat. Carefully brown the lamb on all sides, about 15 minutes. Set aside.

Heat the remaining 2 tablespoons olive oil in a *caldero* or cast-iron kettle large enough to hold the lamb and all the vegetables. Add the vegetables and brown them, about 10 minutes. Add the lamb to the pot and stir with a large spoon so that it is surrounded by the vegetables, then add the split garlic head, peppercorns, and bay leaves and pour in the red wine. The liquid should completely cover the meat; if necessary, add some water. Bring to a boil, skimming any foam that rises to the top, then reduce the heat as low as possible and cook at a bare simmer, uncovered, for 7½ hours, or until the lamb is falling-apart tender. The liquid should be just shuddering with an occasional bubble; check the meat from time to time, and turn it over if it looks dry. If your lamb is very tender after just 4½ hours or so, turn off the heat, cover the pot, and let the meat sit in the liquid for the remaining time.

Remove the lamb from the pot and strain the braising liquid through a fine-mesh strainer into a large saucepan, pushing down on the vegetables with the back of a wooden spoon. Skim off the fat. You should have about 8 cups of liquid. Bring to a boil over high heat and reduce the liquid to about 5 cups, skimming off any fat. Adjust the seasoning with salt and pepper.

Transfer the lamb to a pot, add the reduced braising liquid, and bring to a simmer. Simmer gently until the lamb is heated through.

To serve, slice the lamb and arrange on a deep platter. Spoon the juices over the meat.

# Flipped-and-Flapped Lamb with Mustard, Oregano, and Lemon Confit

I wanted to create a dish that would have all the flavors of a classic French *gigot à la moutarde* (leg of lamb with mustard) but could be prepared in a matter of minutes. Pounding the sliced lamb to make it thinner was the solution.

I was very pleased when Pierre Troisgros, the great French chef for whom I had worked in the early 1980s, came into the restaurant one day. He didn't remember me, but then why should he?—I was just a boy, and he was the most famous chef in the world. I was thrilled when he complimented me on this dish, in particular its simplicity. | Serves 4

**2 pounds butterflied leg of lamb, in one piece**
**Coarse salt and freshly ground black pepper**
**½ cup Dijon mustard**
**½ cup packed fresh oregano leaves, finely chopped**
**1 tablespoon roughly chopped Lemon Confit (page 259)**
**1 tablespoon extra virgin olive oil**

Cut the lamb across the grain into 1-inch-thick slices. Place each one between two sheets of plastic wrap and pound to an even thickness of ½ inch.

Lay the steaks out on a tray, season with salt and pepper to taste, and brush with half the mustard. Turn, season, and coat with remaining mustard. Scatter the chopped oregano and lemon confit evenly over the top.

Brush a *chapa* or large cast-iron skillet with oil and place over high heat (use two pans if you have them). When the pan begins to smoke, add the steaks, oregano and lemon side down, and cook for 3 minutes, without moving. You will smell the mustard and oregano as they brown and form a crust. Use a wide thin spatula to carefully release the steaks, flip them to the other side, and cook for about 2 minutes more, or until done to taste.

# Smashed Patagonian Lamb with Lemon Confit and Herbs

Smashing the lamb steaks and grilling them on hot cast iron produces crusty and succulent meat. A powerful combination of fresh herbs and lemon confit adds a boost of flavor. I've made this with shoulder chops many times, but leg steaks, which are beginning to appear in U.S. markets, are perfect. | Serves 8

¼ **cup minced Lemon Confit (page 259),**
 **plus 2 tablespoons oil from the confit**
¼ **cup fresh oregano leaves, minced**
¼ **cup fresh thyme leaves, minced**
**Coarse salt**
**2 teaspoons crushed red pepper flakes**
**8 bone-in lamb leg steaks (or substitute shoulder**
 **chops), about ¾ inch thick, 7 ounces each**

Combine the lemon confit and herbs in a mortar or a small bowl, and crush them together with the pestle or a wooden spoon. Add the lemon oil, salt to taste, and the red pepper flakes and crush and mash until they form a paste.

Place the lamb steaks on a work surface and smash them lightly around the center bone with a meat pounder so they are of even thickness. Spoon some of the lemon herb mixture onto each steak and rub in well. Cover with plastic wrap and let the flavors penetrate the meat for about 30 minutes at room temperature. (The steaks can be seasoned a day in advance and refrigerated. Bring to room temperature before cooking.)

Heat a *chapa* or two large cast-iron skillets over high heat until a drop of water sizzles on the surface. Add the steaks and cook for 3 to 4 minutes, without moving, until crisp and well browned on the first side. Turn and cook for 3 more minutes, or until done to taste.

# Boneless Pork Chops with Honey Gremolata

London's River Café has influenced me in both its style and its food, which is always made with the most wonderful fresh ingredients. By my standards, Rose Gray is one of the three great chefs in the world (the others being Joël Robuchon and Tetsuya Wakuda, of Sydney, Australia), and she and I have sent young cooks to each other's restaurants a number of times. I owe this recipe to Rose. My contribution is the honey in the gremolata. | Serves 4

**4 boneless pork loin chops, 1 inch thick,**
    **about 8 ounces each**
**3 garlic cloves, grated or minced**
**Generous 1 tablespoon fresh rosemary leaves,**
    **chopped**
**Coarse salt and freshly ground black pepper**
**Olive oil**
**Honey Gremolata (page 255)**

Trim off all the fat and membrane from the meat. Using a meat mallet, pound the pork between two sheets of plastic wrap to an even thickness of ½ inch. Press the garlic and rosemary into the meat, and season with salt and pepper.

Heat a *chapa* or large cast-iron skillet over medium-high heat until a drop of water sizzles on the surface. Brush lightly with olive oil, and when the oil is hot, add the pork, herb and garlic side down. Cook, without moving, for 4 minutes. Turn the pork and cook for 3 minutes more, or until done to taste. The rosemary and garlic should brown but not burn.

Serve with the gremolata.

# Bife de Chancho Wrapped in Prosciutto with Sage

Vanina Chimeno, who runs my restaurant in the Mendoza wine region, got the idea from the Italian *saltimbocca*. *Bife* is our term of affection for a steak, and *chancho* for pig or pork. Get the cast iron very hot so that the pork crisps up well without drying out. | Serves 4

**4 boneless pork loin chops, 1 inch thick,**
    **4 to 5 ounces each**
**Coarse salt and freshly ground black pepper**
**2 tablespoons Dijon mustard**
**12 large fresh sage leaves**
**8 paper-thin slices high-quality prosciutto**
**¼ cup extra virgin olive oil, or as needed**

Trim off all fat and membrane from the meat. Place each chop between two sheets of plastic wrap and pound it to about ½ inch thick. Season carefully with salt, depending on the saltiness of your prosciutto, and pepper. Spread each chop generously with mustard. Arrange 3 sage leaves on each chop so the edges will peek decoratively over the edges of the meat. Cover each cutlet with 2 slices of prosciutto, and drizzle a tablespoon of olive oil over each one.

Heat a *chapa* or one or two large cast-iron skillets over high heat until a drop of water sizzles. Lift each chop with a wide spatula and, in one quick motion, invert onto the hot surface. Cook without moving for 20 seconds, or until the prosciutto crisps. When the prosciutto is very crisp, turn the chops and cook, adding a little more oil if necessary and lowering the heat if the meat starts to burn, until the other side is browned and the meat is done to taste, 3 to 5 minutes. Serve immediately.

OPPOSITE: Bife de Chancho Wrapped in Prosciutto with Sage

# Pork Tenderloin with Burnt Brown Sugar, Orange Confit, and Thyme

One Easter at "the Island," Peter Kaminsky and his family joined me and we cooked, fished, and read for a week. His youngest daughter, Lily, impressed me very much by how very definitive she was about things. To a parent, no doubt, that translated as "picky teenager," but to me it was a young woman with spirit—although I was vexed that she was at that stage where it was hard to persuade her to eat meat.

On the day we returned to Buenos Aires, we lunched at my restaurant. Peter ordered this pork with burnt brown sugar, orange confit, and thyme. To my surprise, Lily requested some and positively devoured it. There's no greater compliment that can be paid to an Argentine chef than converting a non-meat-eater.

| Serves 6

2 pork tenderloins, about 1 pound each
6 pieces Orange Confit (page 259), about 2 inches
    long, plus 2 tablespoons oil from the confit
2 tablespoons fresh thyme leaves
1 tablespoon coarse salt, or to taste
3 tablespoons light brown sugar

Lay the pork tenderloins on a work surface. Tear the orange confit into ½-inch pieces and scatter over the top of the meat. Sprinkle with the thyme and half the salt, then sprinkle the brown sugar on top and pat it down firmly with your hand. Drizzle with the oil from the orange confit.

Heat a *chapa* or a large square or rectangular cast-iron griddle over medium heat until a drop of water sizzles on the surface. Using a wide spatula, lift each pork tenderloin and invert it, sugar side down, onto the hot surface. Cook them, without moving, for 5 minutes. If the sugar begins to smell unpleasantly burned, adjust the heat by moving the griddle and/or lowering the flame. When the sugar side is well browned, turn the tenderloins and cook, turning to sear on all sides, for 10 to 15 minutes more, or until done to taste. The internal temperature should be 135°F for a rosy pink.

Transfer the meat to a carving board and allow to rest, tented loosely with foil, for 10 minutes before slicing. Season to taste with the remaining salt and serve.

Photographs on pages 124–25

PREVIOUS SPREAD: The "Island" at Eastertime, which is our autumn. My "Island" in farthest Patagonia is very remote, but it's the place I feel most at home. OPPOSITE: Lunchtime in Garzon.

Thyme, brown sugar, and orange confit in wonderful olive oil make a simply prepared, complex-tasting crust for Pork Tenderloin with Burnt Brown Sugar, Orange Confit, and Thyme (page 123).

# Peached Pork

The Andes have spawned many legends about "the City That Time Forgot," where the streets are studded with emeralds and philosopher kings reign. Nestled in a mountain valley in Patagonia, the picturesque city of El Bolson, though not lined with jewels, is a bit of a time warp, stuck in the 1960s. It's still a drop-out town offering macramé weavings, wind chimes, and bongs sold by hippie craftsmen who look like they stepped right out of the Summer of Love. Bolson's temperate climate makes it the fruit basket of Argentina, particularly for berries and stone fruits. This recipe, an homage to the region's perfect peaches, is the creation of a gifted young chef, Fernando Hara, who ran my kitchen in Uruguay in the summer of 2008.
| Serves 6

1 boneless pork loin roast, about 2 pounds, butterflied
8 garlic cloves, minced
2 tablespoons minced fresh rosemary leaves
7 to 8 tablespoons extra virgin olive oil
Coarse salt and freshly ground black pepper
6 small peaches, skin on, cut in half and pitted
4 tablespoons unsalted butter, cut into small pieces

Lay the meat out on a work surface and trim off all fat and membrane. Using a meat mallet, pound to an even thickness of ¾ inch.

Combine the garlic, rosemary, and 6 tablespoons of the olive oil in a small bowl. Season the pork with salt and pepper to taste, and spread half of the garlic mixture evenly over the surface. Flip the meat, season with salt and pepper, and cover with the remaining garlic mixture.

Brush a *chapa* or a 12-inch square or two-burner rectangular cast-iron griddle with 1 tablespoon olive oil and heat over medium heat until a drop of water sizzles on the surface. Add the meat to the hot surface and cook until it is well browned and crusty on the first side, about 10 minutes. Meanwhile, arrange the peaches around the meat, cut side down. Dot the butter around and in between the peaches and let them cook until nicely charred on the cut side and slightly softened, about 5 minutes. Transfer to a platter, and cover to keep warm.

When the meat is well browned on the first side, turn and cook on the other side, adding another tablespoon of olive oil if needed, for about 7 minutes, or until done to taste. Transfer the meat to a carving board, tent loosely with foil, and let rest for 3 minutes.

Slice the meat and serve the peaches alongside.

Salt-Crust Roasting

I didn't give salt-crust cooking much thought until the Seville World's Fair in 1992, where I cooked so many steaks that I positively craved a piece of fish. Luckily, La Dorada, one of the great restaurants of Seville, was not too far away from the fairgrounds, and I quickly became enamored of their salt-crusted fish.

A few years later, when I began to focus on wood fire, the salt crust seemed the perfect method for moist, flavorful results, whether using with the massive heat of the *infiernillo* (see page 18) or *horno de barro* (see page 21), or the more controlled heat of a home oven. In much the same way that the thickness of cast iron produces a uniform heating surface, a thick layer of salt transfers heat evenly. Surprisingly, rather than overwhelming you with a salty taste, it produces the juiciest, most delicately cooked meats, poultry, fish, and even vegetables.

Don't be put off by the amount of salt used in this method. (I figure about 3 pounds of salt for every pound of meat.) It really doesn't affect the flavor. In fact, just the opposite: it seals it in and preserves it.

Whole unpeeled vegetables such as squash, potatoes, and carrots are well suited to salt-crust roasting. With fish, meat, and poultry, you also want the skin left on or the salt will penetrate the flesh and draw out moisture. A bone-in fresh ham, with its protective layer

of fat, or a whole salmon or chicken is heavenly when roasted in salt, but I would never want to cook a cut such as a boneless pork loin this way, because it would be dry on the inside and overly salty.

Use a large sheet pan (18 by 26 inches) for larger whole fish or big cuts of meat. For smaller items, such as a whole chicken or bluefish, a roasting pan serves well. In either case, first place a layer of newspaper on the counter, covering an area larger than the pan or skillet, to catch any salt that spills over during the packing process.

Use coarse kosher salt for your salt crusts: Morton's and Diamond Crystal are widely available in 3-pound boxes. Depending on the quantity you need for your recipe, you may need to moisten the salt in batches.

When arranging ingredients to be cooked in salt (or in embers, for that matter), place the larger, denser, longer-cooking vegetables (such as pumpkin or butternut squash) in the center, where the heat is more intense,

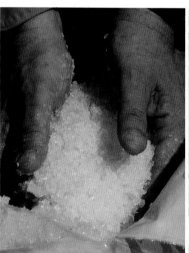

and the smaller, faster-cooking ones (smaller onions, bell peppers, heads of garlic, etc.) closer to the outside.

Because ovens vary and the denseness of the salt crust may vary too (depending on your packing technique), timings in the recipes are meant as guidelines, not commandments. A meat thermometer, stuck through the salt crust and into the flesh just before roasting, will be your best guide.

Put the pan back on the newspaper-covered counter. Be very careful when breaking the salt crust—it is extremely hot. Use a mallet or hammer or a heavy stick to crack the crust, but do it sharply and lightly so that you don't smash the vegetables. Next, using a big, heavy-duty serving spoon with a long handle or wearing gloves, lift off the big pieces and discard them. As the ingredients are exposed, use a pastry brush to whisk away any remaining grains of salt, as though you were excavating an archaeological dig.

And now to the salt-crust pork. Other recipes using this method are Salt-Crust Chicken (page 132), Salt-Baked Striped Bass with Olive Oil, Herb, Lemon, and Garlic Salsa (page 150), and Salt-Baked Salmon on an Infiernillo (page 154), as well as Salt-Crust Potatoes with Marjoram (page 164) and Winter Vegetables Baked in Salt (page 176).

# Salt-Crust Leg of Pork with Honey Gremolata

In this era of factory-bred animals, if your experience with roast pork is one of unchewable dryness, be prepared to be amazed: this is one of the most succulent pieces of pork you'll ever have. You may need help lifting this. | Serves 8 to 10

**24 pounds kosher salt (eight 3-pound boxes)**
**1 leg of young pig, about 11 pounds**
**6 medium potatoes**
**6 sweet potatoes**
**4 large red onions**
**Honey Gremolata (page 255) or Salsa Criolla (page 253)**

Heat an *horno* or home oven (with the rack positioned in the lower third of the oven) to approximately 500°F.

Working in batches, empty 2 or 3 boxes of salt into the sink (or a large basin or bucket if working outdoors). Pour some water over the salt and, using your hands, toss to combine. Add the remaining batches of salt and more water as needed, tossing until the mixture has the consistency of damp snow.

Salt-crust roasting on an *infiernillo*. The salmon recipe on page 154 uses this technique.

Fill a roasting pan or baking sheet with some of the salt and tamp it down so that you have about an inch of compacted salt. Lay the pork leg on the salt. Arrange the potatoes, sweet potatoes, and onions around the meat. Using the remaining salt mixture, cover the pork leg and vegetables, as if you were burying someone in sand at the beach. Tamp the salt down firmly; it should be about 1 inch thick. Stick a meat thermometer (not instant-read) through the salt and into the pork leg. Very carefully transfer the pan to the oven for 1 hour and 45 minutes, or until the thermometer reads 140°F. Spread newspapers on the counter next to the sink. Remove the pan from the oven, place on the newspaper, and let rest for 20 minutes.

Tap the salt crust with a hammer or mallet until it cracks. Lift off the crust and discard it. Remove the vegetables, and brush away the salt. Brush any remaining salt from the pork leg. Cut away the fat and skin, and carve the meat.

Cut up the vegetables, and serve with the gremolata or salsa.

# Salt-Crust Chicken

Food critics often say that the measure of a great restaurant is its roast chicken. This technique is much more forgiving than regular oven-roasting chicken, although it doesn't have a crunchy crust. I believe that achieving moist white meat is even more important than the crust. | Serves 4

**1 chicken, about 3½ pounds**
**5 fresh thyme sprigs**
**4 garlic cloves, unpeeled**
**2 fresh bay leaves**
**9 pounds kosher salt (three 3-pound boxes)**
**Salsa Lucía (page 253)**

Heat an *horno* or home oven (with the rack positioned in the lower third of the oven) to approximately 500°F.

Pat the chicken dry with paper towels. Put the thyme, garlic, and bay leaves in the cavity and truss with kitchen twine.

Empty the salt into the sink (or a large basin or bucket if working outdoors). Pour 2 cups of water over the salt and, using your hands, toss to combine. Add more water as needed, a cup or two at a time, tossing until the mixture has the consistency of damp snow.

Make a 1-inch-deep bed of salt in a roasting pan and tamp it down. Place the chicken in the center. Stick the probe of a meat thermometer into the thickest part of the thigh. Cover the chicken completely with the remaining salt, tamping it down so that it is completely encased.

Transfer the chicken to the oven and roast for 35 to 40 minutes; the internal temperature of the thigh should read 175°F. Spread newspapers on the counter next to the sink. Remove the pan from the oven, place on the newspaper, and let rest for 10 minutes (the internal temperature will rise to about 185°F).

Crack the salt crust with a rolling pin or mallet, lift off the pieces, and discard them. With a pastry brush, brush the remaining salt away from the chicken. Carefully pull off the skin from the breasts and legs. Slice off the breasts from the bone and cut into ½-inch-thick slices. Slice the meat from the legs and thighs.

Arrange the meat on a warm platter and spoon the salsa over the chicken.

# Chicken Chimehuin

I've loved different variations of this recipe ever since my childhood friend Ernest Pfaffenbauer cooked it on a piece of corrugated steel over a lakeside campfire. We would hike along the shores of a lake formed by the crater of an ancient volcano. The Chimehuin River is born there. Among trout fishermen, including the late Jorge Donovan, who's buried beside its waters, this place is mecca, holy water. *Chimehuin* is pronounced as if you are saying "she may win" in English—I like that! | Serves 4

1 chicken, about 2¾ pounds
Coarse salt
Juice of 1 lemon
¼ cup fresh rosemary leaves, minced
1 head garlic, separated into cloves, smashed,
   and peeled
Extra virgin olive oil
Minced Lemon Confit (page 259)
Parsley, Olive Oil, and Garlic Sauce (page 252)

Using kitchen shears, split the chicken down the breastbone and open it out flat. Pat it dry with paper towels.

Season the chicken with salt, the lemon juice, and rosemary; push some of the rosemary under the skin.

Crush the garlic cloves into a coarse paste, using a mortar and pestle or a heavy knife; or grate them with a Microplane grater. Rub the garlic all over the bone side of the chicken, and push some under the skin. Set aside while you prepare the fire (the chicken can be covered and refrigerated for as long as overnight).

Prepare the coals for a medium fire. Or, heat a large, deep-ridged cast-iron grill pan on the stove over medium heat, then brush the ridges well with olive oil.

Place the chicken, skin side up, on the heated grill or in the grill pan and cook until it browns and crisps nicely on the first side, about 15 minutes. Turn the chicken and grill on the other side until the skin is crisp and brown and the chicken is cooked through, 10 to 15 minutes longer.

Cut into serving pieces, sprinkle with the lemon confit, and serve with the sauce.

Also pictured on page 108

The sitting/dining room of Hotel & Restaurant Garzon.

# Chicken Breasts with Capers and Black Olives

Instead of the usual flour or bread crumbs for a crust, there are nonstarchy ingredients that can also serve while adding flavor. Kalamata olives are particularly good because their slightly crisp crust melts pleasantly on your tongue. Also, the type of red wine vinegar used in the Kalamata brine complements the tartness of the capers. | Serves 4

**4 boneless, skinless chicken breast halves,
    about 6 ounces each
Coarse salt and freshly ground black pepper
¼ cup pitted Kalamata olives, finely chopped
1 tablespoon capers, rinsed, dried,
    and finely chopped
2 tablespoons minced fresh oregano,
¼ cup extra virgin olive oil**

Season the chicken breasts with salt and pepper. Combine the olives, capers, oregano, and olive oil in a small bowl. Spoon the mixture evenly over the chicken breasts, pressing it firmly into the flesh with the palm of your hand.

Heat a *chapa* or large cast-iron griddle over high heat until a drop of water sizzles on the surface. Using a wide spatula, lift one of the chicken breasts and, in one motion, carefully invert it onto the hot surface, olive side down. Repeat with the remaining chicken breasts. Cook without moving them, for about 3 minutes, until the olive and caper mixture has charred and crisped nicely. Turn the breasts and cook for 2 more minutes, or until they are cooked through. Serve.

# Fish & Shellfish

# Grilled Scallops with Endive and Radicchio

If ever there was an ingredient that demonstrates the wisdom of the rule "Don't Touch!" (see page 28), it is the scallop. If you leave it alone, it develops a beautiful, delicious crust. If you move it as it cooks, the crust breaks, and the result is watery and uninteresting. Here, the sweetness of the scallops is complemented by the slightly bitter combination of radicchio and endive. | Serves 6

**2 large heads radicchio**

**6 endives**

**7 to 8 tablespoons extra virgin olive oil**

**Coarse salt and freshly ground black pepper**

**30 sea scallops, about 2 pounds, tough side muscle removed, rinsed, and patted dry**

**Parsley, Olive Oil, and Garlic Sauce (page 252)**

**Lemon wedges**

Halve the heads of radicchio, cut each half into 3 wedges, and cut each wedge crosswise in half. Halve the endives lengthwise and cut into 2-inch pieces. Combine the radicchio, endives, 6 tablespoons of the olive oil, and salt and pepper in a bowl, tossing well. Set aside.

Heat a *chapa* or large cast-iron skillet over high heat until a drop of water sizzles on the surface. Brush with 1 tablespoon olive oil, and, working quickly, add the scallops and brown on the first side—it will take only a minute or two. Turn them over, add more oil if needed, and brown on the second side.

Meanwhile, if cooking indoors, heat a second large deep skillet over high heat. Add the radicchio and endives and cook on the hot surface, tossing to wilt on all sides, for about 2 minutes. (If you are cooking outdoors on a *chapa,* sauté the scallops alongside the radicchio and endives.)

Arrange the radicchio and endives on a wide platter. Arrange the scallops on top, so their juices mingle, and drizzle with the sauce. Serve immediately, with the lemon wedges.

Gathering shellfish on the salt lagoon at Garzon

# Cast-Iron-Seared Octopus with Murcia Pimentón

In Spain, octopus is often cooked in a copper casserole and cut up with scissors before serving. I don't know why, but this is traditionally a woman's recipe—I've never seen it made by a man.

I love *pimentón* de Murcia, which is a sweet, pungent sun-dried Spanish paprika, in this dish. Unlike *pimentón* de la Vera, for example, it is not smoked, so its effect is gentler, and it brings out the sweetness in other ingredients, such as octopus.

The octopus should be fresh and tender; frozen octopus can be rubbery. Plunging it repeatedly into boiling water relaxes the flesh before the long simmering. | Serves 4

**2 onions, quartered**
**2 carrots, peeled and halved crosswise**
**2 celery stalks, trimmed and halved crosswise**
**12 garlic cloves, smashed and peeled**
**2 bay leaves**
**Coarse salt and freshly ground black pepper**
**1 fresh octopus, about 1½ pounds, cleaned**
    **(you can have the fishmonger do this)**
    **and well rinsed**
**4 medium red potatoes, scrubbed**
**7 to 8 tablespoons extra virgin olive oil,**
    **plus additional for drizzling**
**1 tablespoon red wine vinegar**
**1 teaspoon *pimentón* de Murcia**
    **(or substitute sweet paprika), or to taste**
**Lemon wedges**

Put a large pot of water on to boil; add the onions, carrots, celery, half the garlic, the bay leaves, and salt and pepper to taste. When the water is boiling, hold the octopus by the head (use tongs to protect your hand and to secure your grip) over the pot and lower the tentacles into the water for 3 seconds. Lift the octopus out and bring the water back to a boil. Repeat the process 2 more times.

Return the octopus to the pot, reduce the heat to low, and simmer for about 1¼ hours, until the tentacles can easily be pulled away from the head. Turn off the heat and allow to cool in the cooking liquid.

Meanwhile, put the potatoes in a large saucepan and add 2 tablespoons of the olive oil, the red wine vinegar, and cold water to cover by about 1 inch. Bring to a boil and cook until the potatoes are tender, 12 to 15 minutes. Drain the potatoes. Gently smash them between paper towels or a dishcloth, keeping them intact, and drizzle with 2 tablespoons olive oil, tossing to coat. Set aside.

When the octopus is cool enough to handle, drain it in a colander. Separate the tentacles (discard the head), and peel away the skin. Toss in a bowl with the remaining garlic, the *pimentón*, salt and pepper to taste, and 3 tablespoons olive oil.

Heat a *chapa* or two large cast-iron skillets or griddles over medium-high heat. Place the potatoes on the *chapa* (or divided between the skillets) and crisp for approximately 8 minutes without moving. Turn the potatoes and add the octopus to sear alongside the potatoes. Don't crowd the ingredients. Sear until very crunchy, about 2 minutes on each side, adding more olive oil if necessary.

Arrange the smashed potatoes on a platter, top with the octopus, and drizzle with olive oil. Serve with lemon wedges.

# Shrimp with Spaetzle

Almost twenty years ago, I was the best man at a wedding on a beautiful farm in Spain. I'd also been asked to prepare the wedding lunch. In church that Sunday morning, the priest delivered a thundering sermon on sin, and my guilty conscience had me thinking he looked at me the entire time. I left the church more than a little concerned for my soul but soon lost myself in the pleasant task of making spaetzle for the forty lunch guests. The only problem was, there was no colander to push the spaetzle batter through. I ended up taking a hammer and a nail to a cracker tin I'd found in the pantry and made my own colander.

The shrimp I serve with the spaetzle could not be more simply cooked, but good shrimp require nothing more than heat to bring out their natural flavor.

While cooking in Italy, I was often told cheese is never included in seafood dishes. This recipe proves that all rules—especially cooking rules—have their exceptions. | Serves 4

**Coarse salt**

**4 cups all-purpose flour**

**Freshly ground black pepper**

**4 large eggs, lightly beaten**

**2 cups water**

**2 pounds jumbo shrimp, peeled and deveined**

**¼ cup extra virgin olive oil, plus a bit more**

**4 scallions, minced, white and green parts kept separate**

**2 teaspoons grated lemon zest**

**2 cups freshly grated Parmesan**

**4 tablespoons unsalted butter**

**Lemon wedges**

Bring a large pot of water to a boil, and add 1 tablespoon salt. Meanwhile, combine the flour, 1 tablespoon salt, and 2 teaspoons pepper in a large bowl. Make a well in the center of the flour and add the eggs and 1 cup of the water. Using your fingertips at first, and then gradually spreading your fingers apart, quickly work the flour into the eggs and water to form a thick, lump-free batter. Season the shrimp with salt and pepper to taste, and toss in a bowl with enough olive oil to coat. Set aside.

When the water is boiling hard, push the batter through a metal colander into the water, using a plastic pastry scraper to force it through the holes. The spaetzle is done when it rises to the surface. Remove it with a large skimmer as it rises and transfer to a large bowl. Toss the spaetzle with 2 tablespoons olive oil to prevent it from sticking together.

Heat a *chapa* or large cast-iron skillet over medium heat. Working in batches, add the remaining 2 tablespoons olive oil and the spaetzle to the pan. Stir in the white part of the scallion and the lemon zest, sprinkle the grated Parmesan over the top, and cook until the spaetzle is lightly browned on the bottom. Turn with a spatula and brown on the other side. Stir in the butter and the scallion greens. Carefully adjust the seasoning.

Meanwhile, if cooking indoors, heat another large skillet over medium-high heat. Add the shrimp and sauté for about 2 minutes on each side, until just cooked through. (If you are cooking outdoors on a *chapa,* sauté the shrimp alongside the spaetzle.)

Transfer the spaetzle to a serving platter and arrange the shrimp on top. Serve with lemon wedges.

Photograph on page 144

# Iron-Box Flounder with Vegetables

Christmas and New Year's are the frantic height of the summer season in Argentina and Uruguay. On a "normal" day at Los Negros, the beach restaurant I had for many years under the lighthouse in José Ignacio, we served 200 lunches. Although I never counted, I would guess that 140 of them were fish cooked in an iron box.

I found my first iron boxes (they resemble a roasting pan made out of cast iron; see photograph, page 20) at a flea market in Brazil. I was looking for a menu item that could be prepared quickly and easily in our new clay ovens, and these fit the bill. I bought fifty of them. If you don't have an iron box for these recipes, you can use a large cast-iron Dutch oven or deep skillet with a lid.

Invite your guests to stand by when you remove the iron box from the oven. (Be very careful not to burn yourself; use heavy-duty oven mitts or pot holders.) Enjoy the oohs and aahs as you take the lid off and the delicious aromas rise with the escaping steam. | Serves 2

1 carrot, peeled and quartered lengthwise

1 medium red potato, quartered lengthwise

1 small sweet potato, quartered lengthwise

1 onion, quartered

2 tablespoons extra virgin olive oil

Coarse salt and freshly ground black pepper

1 small eggplant, cut into wedges

1 red bell pepper, cored, seeded,
    and cut into quarters

1 small zucchini, trimmed and sliced lengthwise
    into 4 wedges

2 large shallots, halved

2 flounder fillets, about 6 ounces each, rinsed and
    patted dry

Parsley, Olive Oil, and Garlic Sauce (page 252)

Heat an *horno* or home oven (with the racks positioned in the upper and lower thirds of the oven) to approximately 475°F. Brush the iron box (see headnote) with olive oil and place on the lower rack of the oven to preheat for 10 minutes.

Toss the carrot, potato, sweet potato, and onion with 1 tablespoon of the olive oil and salt and pepper to taste. Arrange in an even layer in the iron box. Roast, uncovered, for about 5 minutes, or until the vegetables are browned on the bottom.

Remove the iron box from the oven and turn the root vegetables and onion so they brown on the other side. Toss the eggplant, red pepper, zucchini, and shallots with the remaining 1 tablespoon olive oil and season with salt and pepper. Add to the iron box and spread the vegetables out so that they all come in contact with the hot bottom of the box. Return the box to the oven and cook, uncovered, for 25 minutes, turning the vegetables occasionally as necessary. They should be caramelized and tender when pierced with a knife.

Meanwhile, place the lid of the box on the upper rack of the oven to preheat. Season the fish with salt and pepper; set aside.

Remove the iron box from the oven and rearrange the vegetables to clear a space for the fish. Place the fish fillets in the center, cover with the preheated lid, and return to the oven to cook for 4 minutes.

Serve with the sauce.

# Chupin of Salmon and Spring Vegetables

Freshwater fish stews are a specialty among the Native Americans in the northern region that we Argentines call Mesopotamia. They're known as *chupin*—from the Spanish word *chupar*, "to suck," which is what one does to get all the rich juices from the bones. The word *chupin* may also come from the same root as the Italian fishermen's stew known as *cioppino*. Most *chupin* recipes call for tomatoes, but I omit them here. I wanted mine to highlight the greenness of spring and the salmon that run up the rivers in this new season.

| Serves 6 to 8

2 tablespoons extra virgin olive oil

4 large scallions, thinly sliced, white and green
    parts kept separate

4 leeks, white part only, thoroughly washed and
    thinly sliced

2 garlic cloves, smashed and peeled

3 small young carrots, peeled and sliced

2 bay leaves

4 to 5 large fresh oregano sprigs, plus
    3 tablespoons minced oregano

2 cups dry white wine

6 cups fish stock

1 pound red potatoes, peeled, quartered,
    and sliced ½ inch thick

1 cup fresh baby peas

½ cup young fava beans shelled, peeled,
    and lightly cooked

1½ pounds salmon fillet, skin removed and
    cut into 1-inch-wide slices

Coarse salt and freshly ground black pepper

Heat the olive oil in a *caldero* or Dutch oven over medium heat. Add the scallions (white parts only), leeks, garlic, carrots, bay leaves, and oregano sprigs and sauté until the vegetables are golden, about 7 minutes. Add the white wine, raise the heat, bring to a boil, and let bubble for 5 minutes.

Stir in the fish stock and bring to a boil. Add the potatoes and cook until they are tender. Add the peas and beans and reduce the heat to a gentle simmer. Add the salmon slices and poach gently—they will need only about a minute to cook.

Ladle into wide soup bowls, and garnish with the scallion greens and minced oregano.

PREVIOUS SPREAD, LEFT: Shrimp with Spaetzle (page 142).
RIGHT: The front of my hotel in Garzon, Uruguay, in the afternoon sun.

# Brook Trout in Crunchy Potato Crust

About twenty years ago, I built a log house on an island in Lago la Plata, the most isolated lake in Patagonia. It lies at the base of a mountain on the Chilean border, in the middle of the alpine rain forest.

To reach "the Island" requires a six-hour drive in from the coast, the last hundred miles on a dirt road where you can count on at least one flat tire—then an hour's ride on an inflatable launch to the cabin. Among the most beautiful things about this beautiful place are the wild brook trout, all one to three pounds, that teem in the lake. This simple recipe, fillets of trout sandwiched between two potato cakes, was inspired by the crunchy rösti potatoes that the Swiss used to make in Bariloche when I was young. I've made this recipe with many different kinds of fish—trout, flounder, snapper, sole, and others—but in its truest form, it calls for fresh-caught wild Patagonian brook trout, cooked on a lakeside fire.

It's important that the heat is not too high, so that the potatoes crisp up and develop a golden crust but cook through. How long this will take depends on a number of variables, such as the thickness of your pan, the intensity of the fire, and the heating area. Until you get the hang of it, I suggest making a test potato pancake or two before attempting the potatoes with the fish. | Serves 4

**4 tablespoons unsalted butter**
**4 large Idaho (baking) potatoes, peeled**
**4 brook trout, 1 pound each, filleted**
   **(you can have the fishmonger do this),**
   **skin left on**
**1 bunch arugula, washed**
**Coarse salt and freshly ground black pepper**

Heat a *chapa* or large cast-iron skillet over medium heat, and melt half the butter in the pan. Meanwhile, coarsely grate two of the potatoes. Spread the potatoes on the hot surface, making a 1-inch-thick layer. Cook for 10 minutes, or until golden brown and crusty on the bottom. Transfer the potato pancake to a plate.

Melt the remaining butter, grate the remaining two potatoes, and make a second pancake on the hot surface.

Place the trout fillets on the second pancake. Scatter the arugula on top of the fish. In one continuous motion, invert the first potato pancake, crust side up, onto the fillets. Cook for 12 to 15 minutes, or until cooked through. Transfer to a serving plate, season with salt and pepper, and cut into portions, as with a pie.

Photograph on page 148

Peter Kaminsky's daughter Lucy fishing near my mountain cabin.

**OPPOSITE:** Brook Trout in Crunchy Potato Crust (page 147)

# Salt-Baked Striped Bass with Olive Oil, Herb, Lemon, and Garlic Salsa

Although I'm not a fanatical fisherman, some of my closest friends are. Some years ago, to escape the summer heat of Buenos Aires, I gladly accepted the invitation of a true fishing master, Mel Krieger, and the late Jorge Donovan (one of the best friends I ever had and the godfather of Argentine fly-fishing), to be guests of the Menendez Ranch in Tierra del Fuego.

Every day I followed my friends to the Rio Grande. Cold winds from Antarctica howled across the Patagonian steppe. A herd of guanacos—cousins of the llama—grazed on the hills. The southernmost peaks of the Andes, covered with snow, shone in the sun. One evening, while my friends fished, I built myself a campfire on shore.

Mel hooked an enormous trout. Like many fly fishermen, he always releases his catch. I personally think the object of fishing is to catch your dinner, but I respect the catch-and-release point of view. Still, it was a bit frustrating for me to watch so many beautiful meals being set free. Mel told me that he hadn't killed a fish in twenty years. Speaking as a chef, I assured him that tonight we would eat his catch.

I watched him fight the great river beast, drumming my fingers on my skillet in anticipation.

Mel brought the fish ashore. "Well, I caught it," he said, "and if somebody is going to kill it, I suppose it should be me." With that, he finished off the trout and I cooked it.

You may not come across a twenty-pound trout unless you visit Tierra del Fuego, but a freshly caught striped bass or salmon will be equally delicious.

| Serves 8

8 carrots
15 pounds kosher salt (five 3-pound boxes)
1 striped bass, 8 pounds, cleaned but not scaled (see Note)
6 medium potatoes
6 sweet potatoes

FOR THE SALSA
2 cups olive oil
1 cup chopped fresh flat-leaf parsley
½ cup chopped garlic
½ cup fresh oregano leaves
Finely minced zest of 2 lemons
Flaky sea salt, such as Maldon, and freshly ground black pepper

Put the carrots on a sheet of foil and wrap tightly to make a sealed bundle.

Heat an *horno* or home oven (with the rack positioned in the lower third of the oven) to approximately 500°F. Empty the salt into the sink (or a large basin or bucket if working outdoors). Pour 2 cups of water over the salt and, using your hands, toss to combine. Add more water as needed, a cup or two at a time, tossing until the mixture has the consistency of damp snow.

Cover the bottom of a roasting pan or large baking sheet with some of the salt and tamp down so that you have about an inch of compacted salt. Lay the fish on the salt. Place the carrots next to the fish and arrange the potatoes and sweet potatoes around them. Using the remaining salt mixture, cover the fish and vegetables, as if you were burying someone in sand at the beach, and tamp the salt down firmly.

Stick a meat thermometer (not instant-read) through the salt and into the thickest part of the fish. Very carefully place the pan in the oven, and bake until the thermometer reaches 140°F, about 55 minutes. Spread newspapers on the counter next to the sink. When the fish is done, remove the pan from the oven, place on the newspapers, and let rest for 20 minutes.

Meanwhile, make the salsa: combine all the ingredients in a bowl; set aside.

Crack the salt crust with a rolling pin or mallet, lift off the pieces, and discard them. Remove the vegetables. Unwrap the carrots. Brush the salt from the potatoes and sweet potatoes.

Brush the remaining salt from the fish. Gently lift off and discard the skin, then use two large spoons or spatulas to lift the top fillet from the backbone and transfer to individual plates. Remove the backbone and transfer the bottom fillet to plates, leaving the skin behind. Cut up the vegetables and place a serving of carrots, potatoes, and sweet potatoes on each plate. Garnish with the salsa and serve.

NOTE: If your roasting pan or baking sheet isn't large enough to accommodate the whole fish, remove the head and tail.

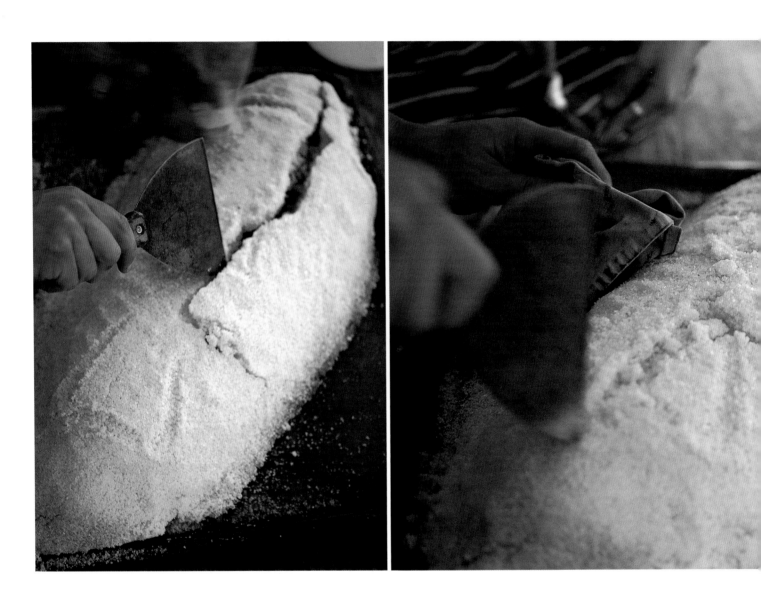

I use a putty knife to lift the salt crust off very carefully. Then I remove one
piece of fish from the bone for each serving.

# Salt-Baked Salmon on an Infiernillo

Making a whole salmon, or any other large fish or cut of meat, on an *infiernillo* is a dramatic event on the program of any outdoor party. I have done this in mountain groves and on ocean beaches, at huge events and (extended) family meals.

The sight of two fires blazing above and below the salt-packed food, which reminds me of a Viking funeral pyre, always draws attention. Preparing a feast this way is not a one-man or -woman job, however. A 15-pound salmon requires more than 35 pounds of salt to encase it. That means that once it's encrusted, the tray will weigh at least 50 pounds.

The other weight-lifting challenge comes at the end of the cooking process. The *infiernillo,* which is really nothing more than one cast-iron table stacked on another cast-iron table, needs to be partially disassembled to get at the fish. The upper level and its fire need to be removed. The best way to do so is to place two crowbars under the top level, gather four strong people to lift it, and move it aside. Whenever I see this done, I am reminded of one of those Easter processions in an old Spanish village when the statue of a saint is carried around the town square by a platoon of men. | Serves 20

One 15-pound salmon
**36 pounds kosher salt (twelve 3-pound boxes)**

FOR THE SALSA
**4 cups olive oil**
**2 cups chopped fresh flat-leaf parsley**
**1 cup chopped garlic**
**1 cup fresh oregano leaves**
**Finely minced zest of 4 lemons**
**Flaky sea salt, such as Maldon, and freshly ground
    black pepper**

Working in batches, empty 2 or 3 boxes of salt into the sink (or a large basin or bucket if working outdoors). Pour some water over the salt and, using your hands, toss to combine. Add the remaining batches of salt and more water as needed, tossing until the mixture has the consistency of damp snow.

Fill a large sheet pan, placed on top of the lower level of the *infiernillo,* with a layer of salt and tamp it down firmly; it should be about 1 inch thick. Lay the fish on the salt bed. Insert a meat thermometer (not instant-read) into the thickest part of the fish. Cover the salmon with another layer of damp salt, leaving the face of the thermometer exposed. Pack the salt tightly so that no moisture can escape.

Prepare the materials for your bottom fire: using branches and logs split into kindling, or logs 2 to 4 inches in diameter, arrange tinder, kindling, and logs under the first level of the *infiernillo*. Do not light this fire yet.

Place the upper level of the *infiernillo* on top of the level that contains the salt-packed fish, and prepare materials for a second fire, as above.

Starting with the top fire, light both fires. (If you use lots of kindling they should catch quickly.) Once the fires are well lit, using a shovel, rake, or hoe, rearrange the blaze if necessary to make sure flames and heat are evenly distributed over the entire surface of each level.

After 20 minutes, shovel all the burning wood, as well as coals and ashes, from the bottom fire to the top level. (Up to this point, the top of the fish will have received only radiant heat from the top fire, since heat rises; now the increased level of radiant heat from the upper level will continue to spread even heat into the mound of salt.) After another 20 minutes, the fish should have reached a temperature of approximately 140°F.

Place two crowbars under the top level of the *infiernillo* and *carefully* remove it, as described in the headnote.

Let the fish stand for at least 10 minutes and up to 1 hour (it won't dry out because no moisture can escape). Meanwhile, make the salsa: combine all the ingredients in a bowl; set aside.

When ready to serve, crack the crust with a sturdy branch or small log. Wear ovenproof mitts as you remove the salt in large pieces. Brush away any remaining salt from the skin. Lift the skin away from the flesh and, using a large spoon or spatula, lift off serving-sized pieces. Serve with the sauce.

For years we never caught fish near "the Island" because my friend Marcial (with whom I built the house) liked to watch them in the lake's clear water.

If you don't want to go to the trouble of making a wooden *a la vara* setup (see page 84), these grill baskets work great for whole fish.

# Salmon a la Vara

On the northeastern border of Argentina, the Tamaco Indians grill all types of freshwater fish *a la vara* using skewers and stakes. I often use this method with a butterflied whole salmon. The trickiest part of the preparation is creating the frame that holds the salmon, but even that looks more difficult than it is. | Serves 8 to 12

**1 salmon, about 8 pounds, butterflied, with backbones and pinbones removed**

About 40 minutes before cooking, build a fire of about a dozen logs. You shouldn't need to add more logs, since the salmon cooks relatively quickly, but you do need a rather large fire so that the heat reaches all the surface area of the salmon evenly.

To hold the salmon open while grilling, weave three sharpened skewers through the flesh as shown in the photograph. For the main support, you'll need a sturdy, straight branch, bark removed and partially split, so that you can slide the salmon onto the support. Fasten the open end of the support by wrapping a few turns of wire around it and twisting to fasten. An oiled long-handled grill basket works quite well if you don't want to construct one made of the branches.

Insert the stake holding the salmon into the ground 6 to 8 feet from the fire, with the skin side facing away from the fire. The heat should be medium-high. If it's too low, the slow-cooked salmon will tend to fall apart. Adjust the heat by leaning the salmon toward or away from the fire. The total cooking time will be about 30 minutes. I like to stir up the fire during the last 10 minutes to get a crispy finish on the salmon flesh.

# Vegetables

# Herbed Potatoes Anna

A classic of French cuisine and a trusted standby in fancy restaurants everywhere. I add chopped fresh herbs and lemon zest to balance the richness of the potatoes. Serve these with A Perfect Steak (page 70).

| Serves 4

2¼ cups melted Clarified Butter (page 255)
2 tablespoons mixed finely chopped fresh herbs
  (thyme, oregano, sage, and/or chives)
1 teaspoon grated lemon zest
4 large Idaho (baking) potatoes, peeled and held
  in a bowl of water
Coarse salt and freshly ground black pepper

Heat an *horno* or home oven (with the rack positioned in the center of the oven) to approximately 350°F. Pour 1 tablespoon clarified butter into each of four 10-ounce ramekins to coat the bottom.

Combine the fresh herbs and the lemon zest in a small bowl.

Slice one potato ¹⁄₁₆ inch thick on a mandoline. Line the bottom of one ramekin with overlapping circles of potato, leaving a small opening in the center. Season lightly with salt and pepper and a sprinkling of the lemon herb mixture, and drizzle with 2 tablespoons butter. Cover with a second layer of potatoes. Lightly salt and pepper them, and add 2 more tablespoons butter. Repeat with another layer of potatoes, season, and sprinkle with some of the lemon herb mixture; drizzle with butter. Repeat the layering, sprinkling every other layer with the lemon herb mixture and using 8 tablespoons butter in all. Press the top layer down every so often so you can fit in more layers, and try to maintain a small gap in the center so that butter can seep down into the potato layers. When the potatoes are about 2 inches deep, give it a final coating of butter, and press down; a little butter should seep out of the layers when you press. Repeat the entire process with the remaining potatoes.

Place the ramekins on a rimmed baking sheet and bake for 40 to 50 minutes, or until the potatoes are brown and crisp on top and tender when pierced with a bamboo skewer. If they begin to brown too quickly, cover with foil.

Run a thin knife or spatula around the edge of each mold to loosen the potatoes, and invert onto a serving plate.

Photograph on page 158

# Potato Dominoes

My favorite potatoes are grown by descendants of Irish settlers near the town of Trevellin in Patagonia. You can always count on Irish farmers for a magical touch with potatoes.

These stacked potato squares look like a line of dominoes that have toppled over. This way of arranging the potatoes and then slow-roasting them yields slices that are well crisped around the edges, slightly crisp on the upper half, and soft on the bottom half.

Start with long Idaho potatoes of even thickness, then trim and slice them just before cooking. Don't rinse or place in water after slicing, or they will lose the starch that is essential for holding the arrangement together and browning the edges.

You can partly prepare an hour or two in advance: Cook the potatoes halfway through (about 20 minutes), and set aside at room temperature. Then return them to the oven 20 to 30 minutes before serving time. The potatoes should be served as soon as they are done, while the slices have varying degrees of crispness; if you let them stand, they will all become rather soft.

| Serves 4

**4 Idaho (baking) potatoes**
**4 tablespoons chilled Clarified Butter (page 255)**
**Coarse salt**

Heat an *horno* or home oven (with the rack positioned in the center of the oven) to approximately 400°F. Line a rimmed baking sheet with a Silpat or use a nonstick baking sheet.

Cut off the two ends of one potato and reserve them. Trim the 4 sides of the potato to form an even brick. Slice the potato about ⅛ inch thick on a mandoline, keeping the slices in order if you can (just like a line of shingled dominoes). Hold the stack of potato slices in the palm of one hand and use the other to shape them back into a brick—as you would a deck of cards. Lay the stack on its side on the baking sheet, and put the reserved potato ends, cut side down, at either end to keep the stack aligned. Then, with the palm of your hand, angle the slices slightly to resemble a line of dominoes that has tilted over. Adjust the end pieces to keep the stack in shape, and align the slices if necessary. Dot the top and sides with 1 tablespoon of the clarified butter. Sprinkle with salt to taste. Repeat with the remaining potatoes, keeping the stacks at least 2 inches apart.

Bake for 40 minutes, or until the potatoes are browned on the edges and tender in the middle when tested with a skewer. Serve immediately.

Photograph on pages 162–63

# Salt-Crust Potatoes with Marjoram

Although potatoes are often treated as a vehicle to soak up the flavor of sauces and more powerfully flavored ingredients, they have their own subtle, delicate taste that begs to be caressed rather than smothered. Marjoram is a perfect foil for this dish of salt-crusted potatoes: it's a calmer cousin of oregano, a gentle, flavorful herb that adds a whiff of sweet perfume.

| Serves 8

**8 equal-sized Yukon Gold potatoes, about 5 ounces each**
**8 large fresh marjoram sprigs**
**8 pounds kosher salt**
**Best-quality extra virgin olive oil**

Heat an *horno* or home oven (with the rack positioned in the center of the oven) to approximately 500°F.

Scrub the potatoes thoroughly. Make a lengthwise incision in each potato and insert a sprig of marjoram in each incision.

Empty the salt into the sink (or a large basin or bucket if working outdoors). Pour 1 cup of water over the salt and, using your hands, toss to combine. Add more water as needed, ½ cup or so at a time, tossing until the mixture has the consistency of damp snow. Make a bed of half the moistened salt in a 9-by-13-inch roasting pan (with sides about 2 inches deep). Nestle the potatoes into the salt, spacing them evenly, without touching the sides of the pan. Cover with the remaining moistened salt, patting it down so that the potatoes are completely encased in salt.

Bake for 30 minutes. Spread newspapers on the counter next to the sink. Remove the roasting pan from the oven, place on the newspaper, and let the potatoes rest for 15 minutes. They will continue to cook inside the crust, but more gently than they would in the oven.

Carefully crack the salt crust, taking care not to break the potatoes, and remove all the salt, according to the instructions on page 131.

Transfer the potatoes to a serving platter and drizzle with the olive oil.

# Sweet Potatoes "Tata" with Honey and Thyme

Everybody has a favorite recipe from Grandma. For me, it's the fried sweet potatoes made by my "Tata" Mercedes Sánchez Ponce de León. She peeled them, cut them into big chunks, and fried them over low heat for a very long time until they were super crisp on the outside and soft and sweet on the inside. This recipe is somewhat different in technique, because I smash the potatoes to get more crust, but it grew out of sweet childhood memories—the sweetness of both the potatoes and Tata. These are great with roast pork.

If you are cooking outdoors, the sweet potatoes can be parboiled in the kitchen ahead of time. | Serves 4

**4 medium sweet potatoes, scrubbed**

**2 tablespoons red wine vinegar**

**2 tablespoons extra virgin olive oil**

**1 bay leaf**

**¼ teaspoon black peppercorns**

**Coarse salt**

**8 fresh thyme sprigs**

**6 tablespoons Clarified Butter (page 255)**

**Freshly ground black pepper**

**2 tablespoons honey**

**1 teaspoon crushed red pepper flakes,
     or to taste**

**3 tablespoons cold unsalted butter,
     cut into small pieces**

Put the potatoes in a large saucepan, add the red wine vinegar, olive oil, bay leaf, peppercorns, salt to taste, and cold water to cover, and bring to a boil. Reduce the heat to medium and boil gently for 12 to 15 minutes, or until the potatoes are tender enough to be easily pierced with a skewer. Drain in a colander; do not allow them to cool, or they will break instead of smash.

Put one potato on a clean dishcloth on a work surface, cover with another clean dishcloth, and using the flat of your hand, slowly and gently smash the potato. Transfer to a tray. Repeat with the remaining potatoes.

Remove the thyme leaves from their stems and reserve both stems and leaves.

Heat the clarified butter on a *chapa* or in a large cast-iron skillet over high heat. When it is hot enough to sizzle, carefully add the potatoes and the thyme stems. Season the potatoes with salt and pepper and cook for 5 to 6 minutes, until well crisped on the bottom. Turn them over, lower the heat, and drizzle the honey over the potatoes. Sprinkle with the red pepper flakes and thyme leaves, and put the pieces of cold butter over, around, and under the potatoes. Cook for 1 to 2 minutes, until the butter melts. Sprinkle with coarse salt and serve.

# Patagonian Potato Galette

I haven't kept count, but I will bet that I have made a million of these. I always serve them under a rib-eye steak and let the warm juices seep into the crispy potatoes. They're good with lamb—in fact, with almost any simple grilled or roasted main course.

In order for the potato slices to stick together they need to retain their starch, so do not rinse them after you slice them—they should go right onto the cast iron. They can be made several hours in advance and kept at room temperature. | Serves 4

**4 Idaho (baking) potatoes, scrubbed and patted dry**
**1 cup melted Clarified Butter (page 255)**
**Coarse salt**

Using a mandoline, slice the unpeeled potatoes $1/16$ inch thick (do not rinse). You will use one potato for each galette; keep the slices of each potato in a stack to prevent them from discoloring.

Heat a *chapa* or 12-inch cast-iron skillet over a low flame (if you have two skillets, make two galettes at a time). Add 2 tablespoons clarified butter to each skillet. Working quickly, lay down a circle of potato slices around the perimeter of the skillet, with their edges overlapping by about ½ inch, angling them slightly up onto the side of the pan, because they will shrink down as they cook. (Do not angle the potato if using a *chapa*.) Continue toward the center of the pan, forming overlapping circles in the same manner, until you have filled the pan; use the smaller potato slices toward the center, and cover the gap in the center with a slice. Spoon 2 more tablespoons of clarified butter around the edges of the galette and over the potatoes, making sure to cover the center. Raise the heat to medium-high, place a heavy pan on top of the potatoes to weigh them down and help them stick together, and cook, without moving the potatoes, for 12 minutes; if one side of the galette seems to be browning faster, rotate the pan and/or adjust the heat if necessary.

After 12 minutes, remove the weight and, using two wide spatulas, flip the galette to cook on the other side. If any potato slices fall out of place, tuck them back in. Replace the weight and cook for 7 to 8 more minutes, or until browned on the second side and cooked thoroughly. Drain on a paper towel and sprinkle with coarse salt to taste. Repeat with the remaining potatoes. Transfer to a heated serving plate and top with a rib-eye steak.

If the galettes are prepared in advance, transfer to baking sheets and warm in a 350°F oven for a minute or two before serving.

# Smashed Potatoes with Tapenade Crust

I particularly like to serve this simple-to-prepare yet complex-tasting dish with full-flavored seafood. For example, it's perfect with the salt-baked striped bass on page 150 because the olives hold their own against the robust flavor of the fish.

When you boil potatoes for smashing, it's important to start them in cold water. They cook more gently that way and are less likely to break up and become soggy. Olive oil and vinegar as well as bay leaves and pepper in the cooking water add subtle flavor. If cooking outdoors, parboil the potatoes ahead of time. | Serves 4

**4 red or white all-purpose potatoes,
    about 5 ounces each, well scrubbed**
**2 tablespoons red wine vinegar**
**6 tablespoons extra virgin olive oil**
**1 bay leaf**
**¼ teaspoon black peppercorns**
**Coarse salt**
**½ cup Black Olive Tapenade (page 251)**

Put the potatoes in a large saucepan and add the red wine vinegar, 2 tablespoons of the olive oil, the bay leaf, peppercorns, and salt to taste. Cover with cold water and bring to a boil. Reduce the heat to medium and cook at a low boil for 12 to 15 minutes, or until the potatoes are tender enough to be pierced through with a skewer. Drain in a colander; do not allow them to cool, or they will break instead of smash.

Put a potato on a clean dishcloth on a work surface, cover with another clean dishcloth, and using the palm of your hand, slowly and gently smash the potato. Transfer to a tray. Repeat with the remaining potatoes. Spoon the remaining ¼ cup olive oil over the potatoes.

Heat a *chapa* or large cast-iron griddle over medium-low heat until a drop of water sizzles on the surface. Put the potatoes on the hot surface, oiled side down, and cook until they are crisp on the first side, about 5 minutes: *don't move them!* Transfer to a tray, crisp side down.

Slide a wide spatula under a crisped potato. Spread a heaping tablespoon of tapenade on top, and press down lightly to compact the crust. With one quick move, flip the potato over onto the hot surface, tapenade side down, and lower the heat slightly. Repeat with the remaining potatoes, and brown them for about 7 minutes, until the tapenade is crisp. Carefully remove the potatoes as they are cooked and invert onto a serving platter, tapenade crust facing up. Serve immediately.

**PREVIOUS SPREAD, LEFT:** When I make my galettes on a smooth, warm *chapa,* the swirling steam wafting from the potatoes is hypnotic. **RIGHT:** The dining room of Francis Mallmann 1884 in Mendoza.

By gently smashing the potato with your palm, you create more surface on which the tapenade can form its delicious crust.

Curanto

Pit cookery is familiar all over the world: in Hawaii, there is the luau, the Maya have the pib, and we have *curanto*. *Curanto* has always been part of a coming-of-age rite of the Tehuelche people of Patagonia. Traditionally, it began when the chief took his place, surrounded by the bare-breasted maidens of the tribe. To attract the attention and win the favor of the young ladies, the young men danced and engaged in feats of horsemanship. All in attendance

sipped a fermented corn beverage. Over the course of eight days of drinking and dancing and even animal sacrifice (involving removing the beating heart from a prize mare), people whipped themselves into an ecstatic and inebriated state. The communal meal was a *curanto* of potatoes, corn, squashes, guanaco (a cousin to the llama), rhea (ostrich), and, in later times, lamb, beef, and pork. In a less wild form, this rite is still practiced by the Tehuelche to mark the first full moon of spring.

This *curanto* calls for lamb, but it could just as easily include a whole salmon fillet, a chicken or two, or any large cut of meat. How much you can make depends on how much your fire pit will hold. If you do include chicken or salmon, serve Salsa Criolla (page 253) or Parsley, Olive Oil, and Garlic Sauce (page 252) along with the chimichurri.

The Tehuelche prepare their *curantos* in a deep pit dug especially for the occasion, but for this recipe, we prepared our *curanto* in a wheelbarrow—which is a lot more practical for most people! To avoid melting the wheel on your wheelbarrow, take it off and prop up the wheelbarrow with cinder blocks or a log.

MENU FOR 8 OR MORE

**1 leg of lamb, 6 to 7 pounds**
**1 lamb shoulder, about 4 pounds (optional)**
**4 large potatoes, scrubbed**
**8 medium beets, trimmed but not peeled**
**4 fennel bulbs**
**8 large carrots, unpeeled**
**Coarse salt and freshly ground black pepper**
**Chimichurri (page 252)**

## 11:30 a.m.

» Put a 2- to 3-inch layer of earth in the bottom of a wheelbarrow, then cover with a layer of rocks 6 to 8 inches in diameter. Start the fire with about 6 logs; as it burns down, add 6 more logs and throw more rocks on top to warm them (never use wet rocks—the steam that results as wet rocks heat up can cause them to explode).

## 1:00 p.m. or so

» When fire has burned down completely, fill the spaces between the hot rocks with coals and embers (photo 1). Shovel another layer of earth, about 2 inches deep, on top of the rocks (photo 2).

» Lay a large piece of burlap or muslin, or a cotton sheet, over the earth. The fabric should be dense enough to protect the food from dirt and large enough so that it can completely envelop the food. Put the lamb and vegetables on the cloth (photo 3). Season with salt and pepper, and fold the cloth over. Lay another cloth over the first one, covering the food completely. Shovel a final layer of earth over it, filling the wheelbarrow and extending a few inches above the rim. Your objective is to have enough earth to trap all the heat.

## 6:00 p.m.

» Carefully remove the top layer of earth, and just as carefully lift the cloth from the food—take your time, making sure to keep the earth away from the food (photo 4). Transfer the food to platters, and serve the lamb with the chimichurri.

1

2

3

4

# Winter Vegetables Baked in Salt

Cracking open a mound of salt and watching the steam waft up is a nice way to add drama to what could otherwise be a run-of-the-mill plate of winter vegetables. Don't be surprised if you need more seasoning at serving time—the baking salt just seals in the flavors; it doesn't permeate the vegetables. Use the very best olive oil. | Serves 6 to 8

**12 to 15 pounds kosher salt (four to five 3-pound boxes), depending on the size of the pan**
**1 butternut squash**
**4 medium beets, trimmed and scrubbed**
**4 large sweet potatoes, scrubbed**
**1 medium red onion, unpeeled**
**1 medium fennel bulb, trimmed**
**3 heads garlic**
**1 small bunch thyme**
**Extra virgin olive oil**
**Coarse salt and freshly ground black pepper**

Heat an *horno* or home oven (with the rack positioned in the lower third of the oven) to approximately 500°F.

Empty the salt into the sink (or a large basin or bucket if working outdoors). Pour 2 cups of water over the salt and, using your hands, toss to combine. Add more water as needed, a cup or two at a time, tossing until the mixture has the consistency of damp snow. Make a bed of salt about ¾ inch deep in a large roasting pan and arrange the vegetables on the salt: put the bottom end of the squash and the larger denser vegetables toward the center and the garlic nearer to, but not touching, the edges of the pan. Scatter the thyme sprigs all around. Cover with the remaining moistened salt, patting it down firmly so the vegetables are completely encased.

Bake for 30 minutes. Remove from the oven and allow the vegetables to rest for 15 minutes.

Place the roasting pan on sheets of newspaper. Carefully crack the salt crust, taking care not to break up the vegetables (they'll be very tender), and remove all the salt, according to the instructions on page 131. With a large spoon, carefully remove the vegetables one by one, brushing off the salt with a pastry brush.

Cut the butternut squash lengthwise in half, spoon out the seeds and fibers, and cut lengthwise in half again. Quarter the beets. Cut both the onion and fennel in half, remove the tough outer layers, and cut in half again. Slice a cross into each sweet potato, and gently squeeze the ends toward the center to expose and push up the flesh. Cut the garlic heads crosswise in half.

Arrange the vegetables on a large platter, scatter the thyme around, and drizzle good olive oil over all. Serve immediately, with a small bowl of coarse salt and a pepper mill.

# Burnt Fennel and Zucchini with Parmesan, Lemon, and Basil

When I was in my twenties, I began to play around with the idea for this recipe on my days off from San Domenico, a Michelin three-star restaurant in Imola in northern Italy, a town well known for its Formula 1 auto races. This salad is a lovely appetizer, but it's also a nice side dish for anything with big flavors, such as Bife de Chancho Wrapped in Prosciutto with Sage (page 118). | Serves 8

**4 small fennel bulbs, about 5 ounces each, trimmed**

**½ cup extra virgin olive oil**

**Coarse salt and freshly ground black pepper**

**4 zucchini, about 4 ounces each, trimmed**

**4 ounces Parmesan cheese, chipped into ½-inch pieces**

**1 teaspoon minced lemon zest**

**2 tablespoons fresh lemon juice**

**½ cup fresh basil leaves**

**½ cup fresh oregano leaves**

Cut the fennel bulbs lengthwise in half. With a sharp knife or a mandoline, slice the fennel lengthwise into very thin slices (⅛ inch thick is ideal). Combine in a bowl with 3 tablespoons of the olive oil and salt and pepper to taste.

With the mandoline or knife, slice the zucchini into rounds about ⅓ inch thick. Toss in a second bowl with 2 tablespoons of the olive oil and salt and pepper to taste.

Heat a *chapa* or large cast-iron skillet over very high heat. When it is very hot, add half the fennel slices and cook for 2 to 3 minutes on the first side, until well charred. Turn and cook on the other side until charred on the outside and tender within. Transfer to a wide serving bowl.

Char the zucchini slices in the same manner. Add to the fennel and toss gently.

Add the chipped Parmesan, lemon zest, and lemon juice and toss. Slice the basil into chiffonade and roughly chop the oregano. Add the herbs to the bowl and toss again. Check the seasoning, and drizzle with the remaining 3 tablespoons olive oil.

# Caramelized Endives with Vinegar

In Patagonia we grow endives, buried in sand. I believe that somehow the leaves capture the crispness of Andean nights. This simple recipe is sweet, sour, and a little smoky. Serve alongside steaks or chops. It's also superb with roast chicken—or roast anything, for that matter. And the caramelized sugar looks gorgeous.

The vinegar gives the dish a delicate tartness, but you can halve the amount if you prefer a less bracing taste. | Serves 4

½ **cup red wine vinegar**
4 **medium endives, trimmed**
⅓ **cup sugar**

Heat a *chapa* or large cast-iron skillet over medium-high heat.

Meanwhile, pour the vinegar into a shallow bowl. Cut the endives lengthwise in half. Dip the cut side in the vinegar and turn to coat. Reserve the vinegar.

Sprinkle the sugar evenly over the hot cooking surface. When the sugar begins to melt, place the endive halves cut side down on the hot surface—do not move for 5 minutes. The sugar will bubble and caramelize; lower the heat if it starts to burn. When the endives are nicely caramelized on the cut side, turn to the other side, pour the remaining vinegar around them (not over them, or you will dissolve the caramelized sugar), and cook for about 3 more minutes, until they are tender and glazed.

NOTE: After removing the endives and liquid, douse the still-hot cooking surface with hot water and scrape so that the sugar doesn't harden on the bottom. It will be *much* easier to clean later.

# Burnt Tomato Halves

Burnt tomatoes are an example of a miracle of culinary alchemy, the Maillard reaction. Discovered by Camille Maillard in 1912, it is a chemical transformation that accounts for the nutty taste of bread crust, the crunchy meatiness of a rib-eye steak, or the deep funky flavor of an aged ham. Burnt tomatoes—especially the deep red beauties from nearby Uruguay—are an ideal garnish for any grilled fish or meat, and they add life to basic pasta sauce. | Serves 4

**4 firm but ripe tomatoes**
**Extra virgin olive oil**
**Coarse salt**
**16 black peppercorns (see Note)**
**2 tablespoons fresh oregano leaves**

Heat a *chapa* or large cast-iron skillet over high heat until a drop of water sizzles on the surface. Meanwhile, cut the tomatoes in half. Brush the cut side of the tomato halves with olive oil and sprinkle with coarse salt to taste.

Place the tomatoes cut side down on the hot surface. Do not move for 8 to 10 minutes, or they will burst and lose their shape. The bottoms of the tomatoes will show a thin black line of char all around when they are done.

Using a sharp-edged spatula, lift the tomatoes off the hot surface and invert onto a serving plate, so that the burnt side is up. With a chef's knife, cut crosshatches into the surface of the tomatoes. Sprinkle with the peppercorns and oregano, drizzle with more olive oil, and serve immediately.

NOTE: I like whole peppercorns here, but if you find them problematic, coarsely crack or grind them.

My collection of French cookbooks occupies a prominent wall in the sitting/dining room of Patagonia Sur, my home and restaurant in Buenos Aires.

# Stacked Ratatouille

When I saw the movie *Ratatouille*, it reminded me of the years I spent in some of the great kitchens of France. Even though the film was a cartoon, I thought it was so true to the life of a chef. I was delighted when Rémy the rat/master chef created a beautifully composed ratatouille rather than the delicious hodgepodge that characterizes the classic recipe—it was the same thing I had been doing! Although I'm against overly prettified restaurant food, I always thought that this way was both easy and elegant, so why not?

I'm not accusing Monsieur Rémy the rat of stealing any of my recipes. I think it's just a case of two chefs thinking along the same lines, and I'm proud to be in such good company. Actually, make that three chefs, because Thomas Keller, the genius of the French Laundry, was the one who thought it up for the Disney movie. | Serves 4 to 6

4 ripe plum tomatoes
2 thick zucchini (about the same diameter
    as the tomatoes)
2 long narrow Asian eggplants
    (about the same diameter as the tomatoes)
¼ cup extra virgin olive oil
Coarse salt and freshly ground black pepper
¼ cup fresh oregano leaves
4 cups fresh baby spinach, lightly steamed
2 tablespoons Lemon Confit (page 259), slivered,
    plus 2 tablespoons oil from the confit

Heat an *horno* or home oven (with the rack positioned in the lower third of the oven) to approximately 400°F.

Slice the tomatoes, zucchini, and eggplants into disks ¼ to ⅓ inch thick. Toss each vegetable in a separate bowl with 1 tablespoon of the olive oil and season to taste with salt and pepper.

Oil a large nonstick roasting pan with the remaining tablespoon of olive oil. Working in batches, stack alternate disks of the three vegetables in the palm of your hand, like playing cards, and lay the stacks on their sides in the roasting pan to make long rows (think of a pack of Life Savers); prop up each end with a ball of aluminum foil. Sprinkle the oregano leaves over the top and press them in between the vegetables.

Bake for about 20 minutes, or until the vegetables are tender all the way through. While the ratatouille is baking, combine the spinach, lemon confit, and lemon oil in a bowl. To serve, place a vegetable stack on each plate and garnish with the spinach.

# Light Meals
# & Salads

# Chivito

According to legend, a great chef in Punta del Este, Uruguay, Antonio Carbonada, had an Argentine lady as a regular customer. One day she asked for her favorite sandwich made with goat (*chivito* in Spanish). There was no goat to be had, so the chef threw together what was on hand—steak, ham, cheese, lettuce, and mayonnaise—and the *chivito* was born. It is now found everywhere in Uruguay.

As with most traditional comfort food, everybody makes their *chivito* just a little differently. Here's mine.

| Serves 4

1 boneless rib steak, 1 pound,
    sliced horizontally into 4 thin steaks
    (you can ask the butcher to do this)
Coarse salt
4 sandwich rolls
½ cup Aioli (page 251)
Four ⅛-inch-thick slices pancetta
2 tablespoons olive oil
4 large eggs
4 slices boiled ham (about 4 ounces)
4 ounces queso blanco or Monterey Jack,
    sliced ¼ inch thick
4 Boston lettuce leaves
2 tomatoes, sliced
2 Roasted Peppers (page 261)

Pound the steaks lightly with a meat mallet until they are evenly about ¼ inch thick. Sprinkle with salt to taste.

Split the rolls and spread aioli on both halves; set aside.

Heat a *chapa* or a two-burner cast-iron griddle over medium-high heat. As it is heating, crisp the pancetta on it, turning once; set aside. When the *chapa* is hot enough that a drop of water sizzles on the surface, add the steaks and cook, without moving, for 2 minutes. Turn and cook for another minute, or until done to taste.

Meanwhile heat the olive oil until it shimmers, then fry the eggs until the whites are cooked but the yolks are still runny.

Place a steak on the bottom half of each of the rolls and top with a slice each of ham, cheese, and crisp pancetta and a fried egg. Cover the other halves with the lettuce, tomatoes, and roasted pepper, and close the sandwiches. Slice in half and serve.

# Pan Bread with Griddled Red Onions and Rosemary

Onions sautéed with rosemary are a sublime combination, particularly with freshly made *chapa* bread, which sops up all the juices. This recipe reminds me of the way the French do liver and onions—just hold the liver!

| Serves 4

**4 large red onions, sliced**
**¼ cup extra virgin olive oil**
**2 tablespoons fresh rosemary leaves,**
    **or more to taste**
**Coarse salt and freshly ground black pepper**
**4 freshly made Chapa Breads (page 248), split**

Combine the sliced onions in a bowl with the olive oil and rosemary, tossing gently. Season to taste with salt and pepper.

Heat a *chapa* or large cast-iron skillet over medium-high heat until a drop of water sizzles on the surface. Add the onions and cook on the first side for 3 to 4 minutes, or until well browned. Turn and cook on the other side for another 2 to 3 minutes, until the onions are tender.

Check the seasoning, and fill the breads with the onions. Cut the sandwiches in half and serve immediately.

# Salmon and Charred Fennel with Aioli on Whole Grain Bread

My hometown of Bariloche gained fame as a ski center, thanks in large part to the enthusiastic efforts of our family friend Jo Hardt, a passionate skier. He put in lifts, cut trails, and attracted people to our town. Breakfast at his home was very German, with dark breads, half a dozen homemade jams, fresh butter and cream, every kind of cold cut, and, always, salmon. I have a very vivid memory—I must have been eight years old at the time—of the way he would wink as he mischievously jabbed two fingers into one of my mother's famous chocolate cakes and licked them clean. My mother pretended not to mind his lapse in table manners. This sandwich is a nod to those Sunday breakfasts at his home. | Serves 4

**1 pound salmon fillet, cut from the thick end, skin removed**
**¼ cup extra virgin olive oil**
**2 fennel bulbs, about 5 ounces each, trimmed**
**Coarse salt and freshly ground black pepper**
**4 whole-grain sandwich rolls**
**Aioli (page 251)**
**One bunch arugula, trimmed, washed, and dried**

Rinse the salmon fillet and pat it dry. Cut into ½-inch-thick slices, and toss with half the olive oil.

Cut the fennel bulbs in half from root to stem, trim the cores, and slice into fine julienne. Sprinkle with salt and pepper and toss with the remaining olive oil.

Heat a *chapa* or large cast-iron skillet over high heat. Working in batches, if necessary, add the fennel, in a thin even layer and cook, turning once or twice, until lightly charred. Transfer to a plate and set aside.

Wipe off the cooking surface. Add only as many salmon slices as will fit in one layer without crowding: they will cook very quickly, about a minute on each side. Transfer to a plate and continue with the rest.

Split the rolls and lightly toast them. Spread the bottom halves with aioli. Cover the bottom of each roll with a layer of arugula, and follow with a layer of charred fennel. Top with the salmon slices, and additional aioli if desired, and close the sandwiches. Serve.

# Patagonian King Crab, Potato, Corn, and Leek Cakes

The Incas in the north of Argentina often cook potatoes and corn together. I thought about this combination when the great Mendoza winemaker Manuel Mas asked me to prepare a luncheon for the release of his 1996 Finca la Anita Syrah. To match the wine, king crab from Tierra del Fuego spoke to me.

Corn and potatoes go well with shellfish, as any New England chowder lover will tell you. As a bit of cooking serendipity, I love the way you see the tracing of the caramelized leeks when you flip the cakes over.

| Serves 4

4 large Idaho (baking) potatoes, peeled

Coarse salt

2 ears fresh sweet corn, husked

8 large egg yolks

2 cups freshly grated Parmesan cheese

Freshly ground black pepper

8 ounces king crab leg meat
   (or substitute snow crab)

¼ cup extra virgin olive oil

2 large leeks, white part only, washed thoroughly
   and thinly sliced on the diagonal

Cut the potatoes into large pieces, put in a large pot of lightly salted cold water, and bring to a boil. Reduce heat to medium and boil gently until the potatoes are completely tender, about 20 minutes.

Meanwhile, boil or steam the corn for several minutes, until tender. Scrape the cooked kernels from the cob; you need ⅔ cup.

Drain the potatoes thoroughly, and mash to a fine puree. Beat in the egg yolks, Parmesan, and 1 teaspoon pepper. Stir in the corn and adjust the seasoning with salt and more pepper if necessary.

Heat a *chapa* or one or two cast-iron skillets over medium heat. Dry the crab well with paper towels. For each cake, pour a tablespoon of olive oil onto the cooking surface, then mound one-quarter of the sliced leeks on top. Place one-quarter of the crab over the leeks and season with salt and pepper. Cover with one-quarter of the potato puree and cook, without moving, for about 5 minutes; the cake should be well browned on the bottom. Using a thin wide spatula, flip the cake on to the other side—do not worry if it gets a little messy, just push it back into shape with the spatula. Raise the heat and brown the potatoes for about a minute. If working indoors, transfer to a baking sheet and keep warm in a 200°F oven while you cook the remaining cakes.

Transfer the crab cakes to individual plates and serve.

# King Crab Salad with Fennel

Tierra del Fuego has some of the very best king crab in the world, but in my early restaurant days, it was difficult to get good-quality ones, because by law they had to be cooked on the fishing boats before landing. One day I was taping a TV show in Ushuaia, a port on the west side of Tierra, on a crab boat. It was a rough day at sea and the captain and crew were very occupied keeping us afloat, so nobody paid much attention to the crabs that were boiling away. After an hour and a half, the poor fellows were very sorry looking, and spongy to boot.

Largely because of the protests of the chefs of Argentina and Chile, who knew that crabs did not have to be so insipid tasting, the boats can now ship chilled, fresh (not cooked) crabs.

If you can't find fresh Patagonian king crab, substitute frozen snow crab or Alaskan king crab legs, shelled and patted dry on paper towels, or large lump crabmeat (already cooked). | Serves 4

1 large fennel bulb, about 12 ounces

2 celery stalks

¼ cup drained Lemon Confit (page 259), slivered

¼ cup lemon juice

½ teaspoon crushed red pepper flakes

Coarse salt

2 teaspoons sugar, or to taste

1 large bunch watercress, trimmed, washed, and dried

12 ounces king crabmeat

5 tablespoons extra virgin olive oil

Trim the fennel bulb and split it in half. Remove the core and slice it into fine julienne on a mandoline (or use a very sharp knife to slice the fennel and celery). Cut the celery diagonally on the mandoline into long paper-thin slices. Toss the fennel and celery slices in a bowl with the lemon confit, lemon juice, the crushed red pepper flakes, coarse salt to taste, and sugar.

Make a bed of watercress on a serving platter. Arrange the fennel and celery over the watercress and drizzle the remaining lemon-confit mixture over it.

Heat a *chapa* or large cast-iron skillet over very high heat until a drop of water sizzles on the surface. Toss the crab with the olive oil and a little salt in a bowl. Quickly sear the crab, on one side only, until just cooked through, 1 to 1½ minutes, depending on the size of the pieces; or sear just until heated through if it is precooked.

Arrange the crab over the salad and serve immediately.

# Tomiticán

## Tomato and Bread Soup with Poached Eggs

I owe this recipe to Connie Aldao. She was the chef some years ago at my restaurant in Mendoza. One night, after a few months working in our office, she asked if she could stay after hours to help in the kitchen. She ended up putting in sixteen-hour days and learned how to cook beautifully. She told me she first tasted *tomaticán* with a local family; then she refined it for the restaurant. I like the roughness of the technique, and especially the way you poach the egg in a space that you clear in the thick soup. | Serves 6

2 cups extra virgin olive oil

1 head garlic, separated into cloves, 3 cloves left
    unpeeled, remaining cloves peeled and minced

10 ounces day-old Pan de Campo (page 243),
    torn into 1-inch pieces

¼ cup minced onion

2 tablespoons minced fresh oregano leaves

2 small dried hot chile peppers or ½ teaspoon
    crushed red pepper flakes

1 bay leaf

8 large ripe tomatoes, peeled and coarsely chopped

Coarse salt and freshly ground black pepper

½ teaspoon sugar, or to taste

1 cup dry white wine

2 teaspoons red wine vinegar

6 large eggs

Heat the olive oil in a *caldero* or large Dutch oven over medium-high heat. Add the 3 whole garlic cloves and the bread and fry the bread for about 5 minutes, turning it carefully and adjusting the heat if necessary, until crisp and golden brown on all sides. Do not break up the bread as it cooks—you want it to retain a crunchy texture. With a slotted spoon, transfer the bread to a bowl and discard the garlic cloves. Pour off all but ¼ cup of the oil (if the oil tastes clean, not burnt, strain it through a fine-mesh sieve and reserve for another use), and return the pot to medium heat.

Add the minced onion, minced garlic, oregano, dried chile peppers or red pepper flakes, and bay leaf and sauté for 3 minutes, until the onion softens. Add the tomatoes, stirring to combine with a wooden spoon. Season with salt and pepper to taste, add the sugar, and cook for 3 minutes. Add the wine, raise the heat, and bring to a boil; let it bubble for 5 minutes to cook off the alcohol. Add the vinegar and cook for 5 more minutes to blend the flavors.

Add the fried bread, lower the heat, and simmer for about 5 minutes, until you have a coarse, thick mass. Again, do not break up the bread—you want it to retain some texture. Remove the bay leaf and whole chile peppers, if you used them. Adjust the seasoning with salt, pepper, and/or sugar.

Make 6 wells in the soup, and break an egg into each. Cover the pot and cook for about 4 minutes, or until the whites are set but the yolks are still runny.

With a large shallow ladle or a serving spoon, carefully scoop out the poached eggs and place one in the bottom of each serving bowl. Ladle the soup around them, and serve immediately.

Photograph on page 184

# Omelet Gramajo

You'll find this on the menu in just about every Argentine bodega and café. According to legend it was invented by Artemio Gramajo, the aide de camp to President Julio Roca in the late nineteenth century. But my grandmother Tata says everyone knows that it was created by Arturito Gramajo, the husband of the great tango singer Elisita Gramajo. What everyone doesn't know is that Arturito courted my grandma in 1919. As a chef, I like to think that my almost-grand-father deserves the credit. It's very important that you have a thin, crisp julienne of potatoes: it's what makes the dish special. | Serves 4

2 red potatoes, about 6 ounces each, scrubbed
2 cups vegetable oil, for frying
2 tablespoons extra virgin olive oil
4 thin slices *jamón ibérico* or other top-quality
   air-dried ham, such as serrano or prosciutto
4 large eggs
Coarse salt and freshly ground black pepper

Using a mandoline or a sharp knife, cut the potatoes into fine julienne.

Heat the vegetable oil in a 10-inch cast-iron skillet or Dutch oven to 360°F. Add the potatoes, in batches if necessary, and cook for about 2 minutes, until golden. Remove with a slotted skimmer and drain on paper towels.

Heat 1 tablespoon of the olive oil in a *chapa* or 12-inch cast-iron skillet over medium heat. Add the ham and crisp for about 15 seconds. Remove to paper towels to drain.

Heat the remaining 1 tablespoon olive oil on the same cooking surface over medium heat. Lightly beat the eggs and pour them in. Flip in the edges with a spatula as the eggs cook to allow the uncooked portion to reach the pan surface. The eggs should be golden on the bottom—if necessary, lower the heat so that they do not brown. When the omelet is set on the bottom but still slightly runny on top, place the potatoes on one half of the omelet, and then the crisped ham. Use a wide spatula to fold over the other half of the omelet, and slide it onto a serving dish. Sprinkle with salt and pepper and serve immediately.

# Springtime Fava Bean Salad with Poached Egg

Last year, while shooting a television series featuring eggs, I decided to add poached eggs, cherry tomatoes, and toast to my standard springtime recipe of fava beans, peas, and pancetta. I loved the result and immediately put it on the menu at the restaurant in Garzon.

Use pancetta or a very mild smoked bacon so as not to overpower the fresh taste of the beans and peas.

If cooking outdoors, fry the eggs instead of poaching them. | Serves 4

**2 cups shelled and peeled very young fava beans**
**6 ounces slab bacon or pancetta, cut into ½-inch dice**
**1 teaspoon red wine vinegar**
**4 large eggs**
**Four ½-inch-thick slices country bread**
**1½ tablespoons extra virgin olive oil**
**8 ounces cherry tomatoes**
**2 tablespoons unsalted butter**
**2 cups very fresh sweet green peas**
**¼ cup tiny fresh mint leaves**
**¼ cup tiny fresh basil leaves**
**Coarse salt and freshly ground black pepper**

Blanch the fava beans in boiling water for 2 to 4 minutes, depending on their size; they should be firm but not hard. Drain and set aside.

Sauté the bacon in a *chapa* or large cast-iron skillet over low heat until the fat renders and the bacon is brown and crisp, about 7 minutes. Remove with a slotted spoon and drain on paper towels. Set the skillet aside.

Meanwhile, bring a saucepan of water to a gentle boil and add the vinegar. Stir the water to form a gentle whirlpool, crack open an egg, and add to the water. Cook for about 3 minutes, until the white holds together but the yolk is still runny. Remove with a slotted spoon and drain on paper towels. Repeat with the remaining eggs. Keep the water at a very low simmer.

Reheat the bacon fat remaining in the skillet over medium heat. Add the bread and fry until lightly toasted on both sides. Transfer to four serving plates.

Wipe out the skillet with paper towels, brush with 1½ teaspoons of the olive oil, and return to medium heat. Add the fava beans and brown for 1 to 2 minutes on one side. With a slotted spoon, transfer to a large bowl.

Add the cherry tomatoes to the skillet, along with the remaining tablespoon of olive oil and cook for 1 to 2 minutes, until softened. Transfer to the bowl with the favas.

Add the butter to the skillet and, once it melts, add the peas and sauté for 1 to 2 minutes, until just cooked through. Add to the favas and tomatoes. Add the mint and basil leaves and toss well. Season with salt and pepper to taste.

Just before serving, carefully add the poached eggs to the saucepan of gently simmering water to rewarm. Drain on paper towels again.

Place an egg on each slice of toast and place on dinner plates. Divide the fava beans, peas, pancetta, and tomatoes among the plates, and serve immediately.

# Pascualina

This dish came to Argentina with immigrants from Genoa. As its name implies, the recipe was originally an Easter specialty, no doubt because of the traditional association between eggs and Easter. The time-honored recipe calls for thirty-three layers of pastry (the number of years Jesus lived on earth), made by repeated rolling out and folding. My version is much quicker. | Serves 6

### FOR THE FILLING

**3 tablespoons unsalted butter**
**2 tablespoons extra virgin olive oil**
**4 onions, halved and thinly sliced**
**2 large bunches Swiss chard**
**8 large eggs**
**2½ cups freshly grated Parmesan**
**Coarse salt and freshly ground black pepper**
**Freshly grated nutmeg**

**1 recipe Empanada Dough (page 57)**
**Olive oil**
**1 large egg, lightly beaten**

Melt 2 tablespoons of the butter with the olive oil in a large skillet over medium-low heat. Add the onions and sauté slowly until they are very soft and golden brown, 15 to 20 minutes. Set aside.

Meanwhile, trim the bottoms of the chard stalks and wash the chard carefully. Trim the stems from the leaves and roughly chop. Reserve the leaves and the chopped stems separately.

Bring a large pot of water to a boil. Have ready a large bowl of lightly salted ice water. Blanch the chard stems in the boiling water for 2 to 3 minutes, until tender. Remove with a skimmer or a large slotted spoon and chill in the ice water, then drain in a colander. Fill the bowl with ice water. Bring the pot of water back to a boil and blanch the leaves for 1 minute, until wilted. Chill in the ice water, then drain and add to the colander with the stems.

Squeeze the chard dry. Roughly chop the stems and leaves together, then squeeze in a cloth to get all the water out.

Heat an *horno* or home oven (with the rack positioned in the lower third of the oven) to approximately 375°F.

Combine the chard with the sautéed onions in a large bowl, mixing well. Beat in 4 of the eggs, one at a time, then stir in 1 cup of the Parmesan. Season carefully with salt, pepper, and nutmeg.

Butter a 10-inch fluted tart pan with a removable bottom. Divide the dough into 3 pieces. Roll out one piece of dough into a 13-inch circle about ⅛ inch thick and fit it into the pan, letting the excess drape over the edges. Brush with olive oil. Roll out the second piece of dough a little thinner and lay it over the first, so that the pan is lined with a double thickness of dough. Press the dough into the bottom corners of the pan all the way around.

Spoon the filling into the pan, smoothing it with a spatula. Make 4 equally spaced wells in the filling and carefully add an egg to each. Cover the top completely with the remaining 1½ cups Parmesan.

Roll out the third piece of dough to a ⅛-inch-thick circle and cover the tart. Trim off the excess dough, leaving about ¾ inch all around (make sure you have three layers and none has gotten caught inside). Pleat the dough (as for Empanadas Mendocinas, page 55) all the way around to seal completely. Decorate the top with pastry trimmings, if desired. Brush the beaten egg over the top of the tart.

Place the tart on a rimmed baking sheet and bake for about 35 to 40 minutes, until the top is golden brown. If it browns unevenly, rotate the pan occasionally during baking. Let cool in the tart pan until the crust shrinks from the sides, then remove the ring and slide the tart onto a platter. Let cool to room temperature before serving.

# Grapefruit Salad with Arugula and Toasted Hazelnuts

Roger Vergé, with whom I apprenticed, created a salad using grapefruit and lobster, which probably explains the genesis of this salad. Vergé was very strict about some things, but as a person, he was very mellow. He taught me that "cheffing" doesn't have to be aggressive: you can achieve superb results with a tender hand.

My vinaigrette calls for grapefruit juice as well as the expected lemon juice. It adds a very different kind of taste and gives this seemingly simple salad a strong identity. | Serves 8

**8 red grapefruit**

FOR THE VINAIGRETTE
**2 tablespoons fresh lemon juice**
**2 tablespoons reserved fresh grapefruit juice**
**Coarse salt and freshly ground black pepper**
**½ cup extra virgin olive oil**

**2 large bunches arugula, trimmed, rinsed, and dried**
**1 cup unblanched hazelnuts, toasted and skinned (see Note) and coarsely chopped**
**¾ cup shaved Parmesan (see Note, page 210)**
**¾ cup Sun-Dried Tomatoes (page 254)**

Using a serrated or other sharp knife, cut off the top and bottom of 1 grapefruit to expose the flesh. Stand the grapefruit upright on the cutting board and carefully cut away the skin and bitter white pith in strips, working from top to bottom and following the natural curve of the fruit. Trim away any remaining pith.

Hold the grapefruit over a bowl to catch the juices and cut down along the membranes on either side of each section to release it, letting the sections drop into the bowl as you go. Repeat with the remaining grapefruit. Transfer the grapefruit sections to another bowl, and reserve 2 tablespoons of the grapefruit juice for the vinaigrette.

To make the vinaigrette, combine the lemon juice, grapefruit juice, and salt and pepper to taste in a medium bowl. Whisk in the olive oil in a slow, steady stream.

Arrange the arugula on a serving platter. Arrange the grapefruit sections over the arugula and scatter the chopped hazelnuts over the top. Drizzle with the vinaigrette, scatter the shaved Parmesan over the salad, and garnish with the sun-dried tomatoes. Serve immediately.

NOTE: To toast and skin the hazelnuts, spread them on a rimmed baking sheet in a preheated 350°F oven and toast for 10 minutes, or until they are lightly browned. Wrap them in a clean dishcloth and rub to remove most of the skin. Return the nuts to the oven for 2 to 3 minutes longer, until they are crisp and fragrant.

# Sheet Music Salad

In Spanish, *carta de musica* means sheet music, but it also refers to a type of paper-thin flatbread. The origin of the bread, however, is not Spain, but Sardinia, the homeland of many of Argentina's Italian immigrants. The flatbread is paper-thin, and it's often painted with honey. I've been serving it with salad in my restaurants for many years and it's one of the most popular items on the menu. Almost anything goes well on a *carta de musica*, so don't be afraid to experiment: Fresh figs or pears, for example, and buffalo mozzarella all work perfectly in this salad. | Serves 6

## FOR THE FLATBREAD
**3 cups all-purpose flour**
**1½ tablespoons salt**
**1 cup tepid water**

## FOR THE VINAIGRETTE
**2 tablespoons fresh lemon juice**
**1 tablespoon honey**
**½ teaspoon coarse salt**
**⅛ teaspoon freshly ground black pepper**
**6 tablespoons extra virgin olive oil**

## FOR THE SALAD
**3 cups delicate mixed greens, washed and dried**
**18 Sun-Dried Tomatoes (page 254)**
**3 tablespoons Toasted Almonds (page 254)**
**6 large thin slices *jamón ibérico* or other top-quality**
 **air-dried ham, such as serrano or prosciutto,**
 **torn (not cut) into 1-inch pieces**
**1 large pear, cored and thinly sliced, or 3 fresh figs,**
 **torn in half, and 6 ounces mozzarella di bufala,**
 **torn into small rough pieces**

To make the flatbreads, combine the flour and salt in the bowl of a heavy-duty mixer fitted with the paddle attachment. Gradually add the water, mixing on low speed. Stop the mixer occasionally, remove the bowl from the stand, and knead the dough briefly by hand to help incorporate the ingredients evenly, then continue mixing with the paddle until you have a uniform dough. Switch to the dough hook and knead for about 8 minutes, until you have a really smooth, stiff dough.

Shape the dough into a ball, place in a floured bowl, cover with plastic wrap, and chill for 1 hour.

Flour a work surface. Divide the dough into 6 even pieces. Work with one piece at a time, keeping the remainder in the bowl covered with plastic wrap. Roll one piece of dough into a little ball between your palms, then use a rolling pin to roll it out in a circle 6 inches in diameter. Put on a plate and cover with plastic wrap. Repeat with a second ball of dough, placing the rolled-out circle on top of the first one and covering it with more plastic. Continue with the remaining 4 pieces of dough. Cover the whole stack with plastic wrap and let rest overnight in the refrigerator.

The next day, remove the circles from the refrigerator and work with one of them at a time, keeping the remainder covered so they don't dry out. Set a 12-inch-wide Dutch oven or deep cast-iron pot over very low heat. Stretch out the first circle of dough by hand, as you would a pizza, until it is roughly 15 inches in diameter and thin enough to almost see through without tearing. One method is to press one end against the edge of the counter and gently pull it away from the counter, then rotate a quarter turn and stretch again; repeat to stretch in all directions. When the dough is as thin as it can get without tearing, drape it over the top of the pot. Heat over a very low flame until the dough is completely dry and feels like parchment, about 15 minutes. Use a sharp knife to carefully cut the flatbread away from the rim of the pot and set aside on a rack. Repeat with the remaining 5 circles.

To make the vinaigrette, combine the lemon juice, honey, salt, and pepper in a small bowl. Gradually whisk in the olive oil in a slow, steady stream.

To assemble the salad, dress the mixed greens very lightly with half the honey vinaigrette. Set a flatbread on each of six individual plates. Top the sheets with the greens. Garnish each salad with 3 sun-dried tomatoes, ½ tablespoon almonds, and one-sixth of the ham, and then with the pear slices or the torn figs and mozzarella. Drizzle the remaining vinaigrette over the top and serve immediately.

Photograph on page 209

**OPPOSITE:** My youngest daughters enjoying a ride in the wonderful car of my friend Martin Summers. **ABOVE:** Sheet Music Salad (page 206).

# Chicken Livers with Artichokes, Arugula, Lemon, and Almond

This dish reflects a little bit of each place that's been significant in my cooking life: the lovely salads of France with soft sautéed livers and crispy croutons; the lemony light salad dressings of Italy; and the local artichokes and almonds that are often in my larder in Argentina. | Serves 8

4 lemons, halved

4 bay leaves

Coarse salt

¼ teaspoon black peppercorns

16 small artichokes, with stems

8 fresh thyme sprigs

8 garlic cloves, smashed but not peeled

6 tablespoons extra virgin olive oil

8 chicken livers, about 1 pound, separated into
    lobes and trimmed

Freshly ground black pepper

2 bunches arugula, trimmed, rinsed, and dried

Lemon Vinaigrette (page 258)

¾ cup slivered almonds, toasted (see page 254)

¾ cup shaved Parmesan (see Note)

Bring 4 quarts of water to a boil in a large pot. Squeeze the juice of the lemons into the pot, and add the squeezed lemon halves, bay leaves, salt to taste, and the peppercorns. Add the artichokes, reduce the heat slightly, and cook at a low boil until tender, about 20 minutes. Drain, reserving the bay leaves and lemon halves, and allow the artichokes to cool slightly.

Remove all the artichoke leaves and scrape out the inedible choke from each one; leave the stem attached, if they are tender. Combine in a bowl with the reserved bay leaves, the thyme, garlic cloves, and ¼ cup of the olive oil, tossing to coat. Let marinate at room temperature for 2 hours.

Tear the lemon halves into quarters. Lay skin side down on a flat surface. With a very sharp knife, scrape away every bit of white pith and pulp, leaving only the zest. Cut into 1-inch-wide strips. Set aside.

Heat a *chapa* or large cast-iron skillet over high heat until a drop of water sizzles on the surface. Add the artichokes, stem side up, and cook for 2 to 3 minutes, until they brown slightly.

Heat the remaining 2 tablespoons olive oil on the *chapa* or in a second large cast-iron skillet over medium-high heat. Add the chicken livers, in batches, and sauté for 1 to 2 minutes on each side, or until done to taste. Season to taste with salt and pepper.

Toss the arugula with half the vinaigrette and arrange on a serving platter. Arrange the artichokes and chicken livers on top, and garnish with the lemon zest, toasted almonds, and shaved Parmesan. Drizzle with the remaining vinaigrette, and serve.

NOTE: Shaved Parmesan adds an attractive look to a salad. Hold a large piece of Parmesan firmly against a cutting board and scrape it with a heavy chef's knife; you will get nice shavings. You can also use a vegetable peeler to shave the cheese.

# Whole Andean Pumpkin Salad with Mint, Arugula, and Goat Cheese

When you cut this roasted pumpkin open, it "exhales" with an impressive puff of sweetly scented steam. The greens, cheese, and vinaigrette are then tossed into the pumpkin halves, which serve as their own salad bowls. The results may look a bit messy, but don't worry, it's always eaten down to the last bite.

You can substitute zapallo or ambercup or other smooth-fleshed squash for the pumpkin. | Serves 8

**1 Andean-type pumpkin (see headnote), about 5 pounds, stem removed**

FOR THE VINAIGRETTE
**2 tablespoons finely chopped fresh mint**
**¼ cup red wine vinegar**
**½ cup extra virgin olive oil**
**Coarse salt and freshly ground black pepper**
**8 ounces Bûcheron or similar goat cheese, cut into ½-inch slices**
**1 large bunch arugula, trimmed, rinsed, and dried**

Prepare the embers if using a wood fire (see page 22), or preheat the oven to 375°F.

Put the pumpkin in the embers and cover it completely. Cook until the temperature in the center registers 150°F. Or put it in a roasting pan and roast in the oven for 40 to 45 minutes.

While the pumpkin is cooking, make the mint vinaigrette: Put the chopped mint in a small bowl. Whisk in the red wine vinegar, then whisk in the olive oil in a steady stream. Season to taste with salt and pepper.

When the pumpkin is cooked, remove from the embers or oven and let stand a few minutes. Slice horizontally in half with a long serrated knife, and use a large sharp spoon to scrape out all the seeds and fibers.

Divide the goat cheese between the pumpkin halves, and put the arugula on top of the goat cheese. Pour half the mint vinaigrette over each salad. Gently scrape the pumpkin flesh from the shells with the spoon, combining it with the greens and dressing. Toss as you would a salad, and serve immediately.

Photographs on pages 212–13

**ABOVE:** Very few vegetable dishes have the drama of slicing a roast at tableside, but cutting open an ember-roasted pumpkin, watching the steam billow, and then tossing the salad ingredients makes for quite a show. **OPPOSITE:** Whole Andean Pumpkin Salad with Mint, Arugula, and Goat Cheese (page 211).

# Burnt Tomatoes and Fennel with Mustard Vinaigrette

I know of nothing better to complement fire-grilled lamb or beef than this rustic, straightforward, powerfully sharp, and tangy salad. | Serves 4

FOR THE VINAIGRETTE
**2 tablespoons Dijon mustard**
**2 tablespoons red wine vinegar**
**¼ cup extra virgin olive oil**
**Coarse salt and freshly ground black pepper**

**8 ounces cherry tomatoes**
**¼ cup extra virgin olive oil**
**Coarse salt and freshly ground black pepper**
**4 small fennel bulbs, about 1¼ pounds, trimmed**

To make the vinaigrette, whisk together the mustard and red wine vinegar in a small bowl. Whisk in the olive oil in a slow, steady stream until thickened and emulsified. Season to taste with salt and pepper. Set aside.

Cut the tomatoes in half. Toss in a bowl with 2 tablespoons of the olive oil and salt and pepper to taste.

With a sharp knife or a mandoline, slice the fennel lengthwise about ⅓ inch thick. Toss in a second bowl with the remaining 2 tablespoons olive oil. Season to taste with salt and pepper.

Heat a *chapa* or two large cast-iron skillets over high heat until a drop of water sizzles on the surface. Working in batches, if necessary, carefully place the tomato halves cut side on the hot surface, spacing them about an inch apart from each other. Do not move the tomatoes while they cook, or they will release their juices and lose their shape and texture. When they are well charred, transfer them with tongs or a spatula to a large tray, charred side up, spacing them apart so they don't steam.

Wipe off the cooking surface with paper towels and heat again over high heat. Add the fennel slices in batches, if necessary, and cook for 3 minutes on each side, or until well charred and tender within. Transfer to a serving bowl.

Add the tomatoes to the fennel and toss gently with the vinaigrette. Serve immediately.

# Crunchy Roasted Potato and Arugula Salad

There are endless variations on potato salad. What I find so wonderful in this one are the crisp outsides of the potato nuggets contrasted with the soft insides. The arugula and almonds accentuate the crunch, and the almonds underscore the nuttiness of the crisped potatoes.  | Serves 8

**8 Idaho (baking) potatoes, about 6 ounces each, scrubbed**
**2 tablespoons red wine vinegar**
**6 tablespoons extra virgin olive oil, plus more if necessary**

FOR THE VINAIGRETTE
**2 tablespoons Dijon mustard**
**2 tablespoons red wine vinegar**
**Freshly ground black pepper**
**½ cup extra virgin olive oil**

**1 large bunch arugula, trimmed, washed, and dried**
**1 cup Toasted Almonds (page 254)**

Put the whole potatoes in a large pot of cold salted water, add the vinegar, and bring to a boil. Reduce the heat and boil gently for about 20 minutes, or until the potatoes can be pierced with a skewer. Drain in a colander.

When the potatoes are cool enough to handle, split them with a fork and crumble into coarse ½-inch pieces. Pat dry with paper towels.

Heat an *horno* or home oven (with the rack positioned in the lower third of the oven) to approximately 500°F.

Heat a *chapa* or two large cast-iron skillets over very high heat until a drop of water sizzles on the surface. (If you have only one large skillet, crisp the potatoes in 2 batches, transferring them to a baking sheet as they are done, then transfer to the *horno* or oven to finish them.) Divide the olive oil between the skillets. When the oil is almost smoking, divide the crumbled potatoes between the skillets, making an uncrowded layer in each, and cook until they form a light golden crust on the bottom. Turn with a spatula, add more oil if necessary, and crisp the other side.

Transfer the pans to the *horno* or oven and roast for 10 to 12 minutes, or until the potatoes are deep golden brown.

Meanwhile, make the vinaigrette: Whisk the mustard and the vinegar together in a bowl. Add pepper to taste, then whisk in the olive oil in a slow, steady stream until the dressing thickens and emulsifies. Set aside.

Put the potatoes on a large deep platter and top with the arugula and toasted almonds. Toss gently with the vinaigrette, and serve immediately.

NOTE: If you have a wood-burning oven, you can crisp the broken-up potatoes entirely in the oven. Lightly coat a baking sheet with extra virgin olive oil, spread out the potatoes on the pan, and brown them in the hot oven. Timing will depend on the heat of your oven.

Photograph on page 216

**ABOVE:** Crunchy Roasted Potato and Arugula Salad (page 215).
**OPPOSITE:** Finca la Anita winery in Mendoza.

Desserts

# Burnt Stone-Fruit Tart

When I started to cook with iron boxes, I looked for ways to use them to make desserts. Charring stone fruit at super high heat in the iron boxes in my *horno* worked beautifully, and I still do that. But now, when I go to a cookout, I get the same effect by charring fruit on a *chapa*.

You can make the pastry shell in advance and bring it along to your cookout—if you do so, return the cooled pastry shell to the tart ring to protect it until you're ready to assemble the tart. Then prepare the fruits on the spot. | Serves 6

### FOR THE TART SHELL
**2 cups all-purpose flour**
**10 tablespoons (1¼ sticks) unsalted butter,**
    **cut into ½-inch pieces and chilled**
**5 tablespoons superfine sugar**
**1 large egg**

**8 to 10 small ripe peaches or plums,**
    **about 2 pounds, or a combination**
**3 tablespoons unsalted butter**
**1 tablespoon peach or plum jam**

To make the tart shell, put the flour in a medium bowl. With your fingers or a pastry blender, work in the butter until the mixture has the consistency of coarsely grated Parmesan. Whisk the sugar into the egg, then, using a fork, work gently into the flour and butter until a dough forms. If the mixture seems dry, add a little cold water. Turn the dough out onto a work surface. With the heel of your palm, push out portions of dough from the center. Gather up the dough with a pastry scraper, turn over, and repeat. Gather into a disk, wrap in plastic wrap, and chill for at least 1 hour, preferably overnight.

Heat an *horno* or home oven (with the rack positioned in the lower third of the oven) to approximately 350°F.

On a floured surface, roll out the dough to a 13-inch circle. Fit it into a 10-inch tart pan with a removable bottom. Fold the overhanging dough over itself all the way around to reinforce the sides. Prick the dough all over with a fork. Line the dough with aluminum foil and fill with dried beans.

Bake for 10 minutes. Remove the foil and beans and return to the oven for 10 to 12 minutes, until crisp and lightly golden. Transfer to a rack. When it is cool enough to handle, remove the ring of the tart pan and place the shell on a serving plate.

Cut the peaches or plums in half and remove the pits (leave the skin on). Heat a *chapa* or large cast-iron griddle until a drop of water sizzles on the surface. Melt 1 tablespoon of butter in the pan and arrange the fruit cut side down on the hot surface. Dot the remaining butter around and in between the fruit and cook, without moving, for 3 minutes, or until nicely burned on the bottom.

Brush the inside of the tart shell with the jam. Arrange the fruit in the shell, burnt side up. Unmold the tart and serve.

# Crepes Soufflées
# with Raspberry Preserves

My brother Carlos and I were partners in a jam factory in Bariloche. He also had a farm, about twenty acres, where he grew strawberries, raspberries, red currants, boysenberries, and our very Patagonian calafate, a beautiful evergreen with purple fruits (known in English as barberries). I was looking for a recipe to promote our products and came up with these tiny soufflés as a perfect platform for red-fruit jams. The factory is long gone, but I still make the dessert. | Serves 4 to 6

**1 cup Crepe Batter (page 234)**
**4 large egg whites**
**1 to 2 tablespoons unsalted butter,**
      **at room temperature**
**About ½ cup homemade or best-quality**
      **store-bought raspberry jam**

Place the batter in a large bowl. In another large bowl, beat the egg whites to stiff peaks. Fold ¼ cup of the egg whites into the batter to lighten it, then gently fold in the remaining egg whites. The mixture should be very light and mousse-like.

 Heat a *chapa* or one or two large cast-iron griddles or skillets over medium heat. Brush the surface with softened butter. Reduce the heat to low and place heaping tablespoons of the batter in separate dollops on the cooking surface, keeping them well

apart from each other to allow them to rise, and let them cook very slowly for 6 to 8 minutes, until they are set and just beginning to turn lightly golden on the edges. Turn them over with a spatula and cook for about 4 minutes more, until they just begin to turn gold on the bottom. Transfer to a serving platter and cook the remaining crepes. Gently top each crepe with a teaspoon of jam, and serve immediately.

# Burnt Oranges
# with Rosemary

Burnt oranges with a sugar-and-rosemary crust is one of my simplest recipes. But the flavors and texture—bitter, sweet, fruity, floral, herbal, and smoothly creamy—are supremely intense and complex. The amount of smoke involved makes this a dish you definitely don't want to do indoors. | Serves 4

**4 oranges**
**2 tablespoons fresh rosemary leaves**
**½ cup sugar**
**1 cup plain thick Greek yogurt**

Cut both ends off the oranges. One at a time, using a sharp paring knife, remove the peel and all the white pith from each orange in strips, working from top to bottom all the way around the orange. Cut the oranges crosswise in half and place them on a plate cut side up.

Sprinkle the rosemary leaves over the oranges, and push some of the rosemary leaves into them so they adhere. Sprinkle half the sugar on top.

Heat a *chapa* or large cast-iron skillet over medium-high heat. Spread the remaining sugar on the cooking surface and when it begins to melt, put the oranges cut side down on the sugar. Do not move them for 3 to 4 minutes, and adjust the heat so that the cut side burns nicely but does not smell acrid and the oranges are softened.

Transfer "burnt" side up to individual plates. Spoon the yogurt next to the oranges. Drizzle the burnt sugar and juices from the pan over the oranges and yogurt, and serve.

Also pictured on page 218

Making the Granny Smith Pancakes on a *chapa*, using uncored apple slices.

# Granny Smith Pancakes

Caramelizing brown sugar creates a sweet yet bitter crust, which contrasts marvelously with the naturally sweet softness of cooked apples. This is a perfect dessert to make on a *chapa* at the end of a cookout, but it's equally wonderful as a country breakfast, accompanied by crisp bacon or *jamón ibérico*.

To flip the pancake, I use a wide putty knife (available at the hardware store), sliding it under the pancake in order flip it in one motion. | Serves 2

**1 Granny Smith apple, about 7 ounces**
**10 tablespoons (1¼ sticks) unsalted butter**
**1 cup packed light brown sugar**
**1 cup Crepe Batter (page 234)**

Core the unpeeled apple, slice into ⅛-inch-thick rounds, and discard the end pieces (see Note).

Heat a *chapa* or 12-inch nonstick skillet over medium-high heat. Add 2 tablespoons of the butter and melt to coat the surface evenly. Scatter half the brown sugar over the butter. When the sugar starts to melt, place half the apple slices in a single layer on the sugar and cook, without moving, for 3 to 5 minutes, until they puff slightly and become deeply browned and caramelized on the bottom. Using tongs, turn the apples and caramelize on the other side for 1 to 2 minutes, then transfer to a tray. Scrape the burnt sugar off the *chapa* or wipe out the skillet, and repeat with 2 more tablespoons of the butter and the remaining sugar and apple slices. Add them to the tray when they are done and clean off the *chapa* or wipe out the skillet once again.

Cut 2 tablespoons of the butter into cubes and set aside.

Melt 1 tablespoon of the butter on the clean *chapa* or in the skillet. When the foam begins to subside, pour in half the crepe batter, using a wide spatula or spackling knife to spread it evenly into a circle. Cook for 1½ to 2 minutes, until the pancake is set and golden on the bottom. Using the spatula or knife, loosen and flip the pancake. Using tongs, put half the caramelized apple slices one by one on top of the batter and dot them with half the cubed butter. When the bottom is set and golden, loosen the pancake with the spatula or knife, and transfer it to a plate (if cooking indoors, slide it onto a plate). Repeat with the remaining ingredients for a second pancake.

Serve immediately.

NOTE: Coring the apples is optional; the photographs show the recipe with uncored apples.

# Leche Quemada

This is a traditional recipe, which I first encountered in a seventeenth-century convent that's been turned into a restaurant in the province of Salta. It's basically a crema catalana or crème brûlée, with extra silky creaminess coming from the crème fraîche. Rather than create a crust under the broiler, or with a small blowtorch, I apply heat using cast iron. It makes for quite a show when you place a superhot cast-iron pan on the sugared surface and it caramelizes at tableside.

| Serves 4

½ cup whole milk
1½ cups crème fraîche
½ vanilla bean, split
6 large egg yolks
1 cup sugar

Heat an *horno* or home oven (with the rack positioned in the lower third of the oven) to approximately 350°F.

Combine the milk and crème fraîche in a small saucepan. Scrape the seeds from the vanilla bean and add the seeds and bean to the pan. Bring to a boil, and remove from the heat.

Beat the egg yolks with ½ cup of the sugar in a large bowl, using a whisk or hand mixer, until they are very light and form a ribbon when dropped from the whisk. Whisking constantly, gradually add the crème fraîche mixture. Strain through a fine-mesh sieve into a 10-inch ceramic pie plate. Set the pie plate into a roasting pan and add enough boiling water to the roasting pan to come halfway up the sides of the pie plate.

Bake for about 30 minutes, or until the custard is set around the edges but the middle still jiggles when shaken. Remove and let cool, then chill in the refrigerator until firm on top.

Just before serving, sprinkle the remaining ½ cup of sugar evenly over the top of the custard. Heat a clean 8- or 9-inch cast-iron skillet (one that will fit on the surface of the custard) over high heat for several minutes, until it is smoking vigorously. With a thick pot holder, lift the skillet by the handle and hold it lightly on top of the sugar, just touching the surface—the sugar will hiss and bubble and begin to caramelize. When the hissing subsides, remove the skillet: the sugar should be browned and crisp on top. Allow the caramel to harden for a few minutes, then serve.

# Dulce de Leche Flan

I make this most irresistible of desserts in my *horno de barro*, which requires that you be intimate and expert with your wood oven, so here's a foolproof way to make it in a conventional oven. Preparing it is a long but basically uncomplicated process that calls for you to make dulce de leche, a version that's only half as intense and reduced as the store-bought variety, so that you can fold eggs into it. The trick is knowing when to stop reducing the sweetened milk. Once you get the hang of it, however, it becomes a skill you never forget.

Start this at least two days before you plan to serve the flan. The dulce de leche, once prepared, keeps for a long time in the fridge. | Serves 16

FOR THE DULCE DE LECHE

**2 quarts whole milk**

**4 cups sugar**

**½ vanilla bean, split**

**1 cup sugar**

**½ cup water**

**2 large eggs**

**14 large egg yolks**

**Unsweetened whipped cream for serving**

To make the dulce de leche, combine the milk and sugar in a large heavy pot. Scrape the seeds from the vanilla bean and add the seeds and pod to the pot. Heat over medium-high heat, stirring until the sugar dissolves and the milk is almost boiling. Immediately reduce the heat to a low simmer, and skim off the foam. Simmer very gently, without stirring, for 4 hours, or until the mixture is a very light coffee color and has a syrupy consistency.

Strain the dulce de leche through a fine-mesh strainer into a large glass measure or a bowl; you should have 4 cups. Let cool, then cover with plastic wrap and refrigerate until ready to use.

Preheat the oven to 250°F. Set a 9-by-5-by-3-inch (8-cup) loaf pan in a roasting pan and pour about 1 inch of boiling water into the roasting pan to make a bain-marie (water bath).

To make the caramel, combine the sugar and water in a small heavy saucepan, set over medium-high heat, and swirl the pan until the sugar completely dissolves; do not stir. When the sugar is dissolved, boil the syrup, swirling occasionally, until it turns a golden amber color. Immediately remove from the heat and pour into the loaf pan, tilting the pan to cover the bottom. (The heat of the water in the bain-marie will keep the caramel from hardening before it covers the whole bottom of the pan.) When the bottom is evenly covered, remove the pan from the bain-marie and allow the caramel to cool for several minutes, until it completely hardens.

Put the eggs and egg yolks in a large bowl and whisk to combine. Add the dulce de leche, whisking to blend thoroughly, then pass through a fine-mesh strainer into the caramel-lined loaf pan. Return the loaf pan to the roasting pan and add enough boiling water to the roasting pan to come halfway up the sides of the loaf pan. Cover the entire bain-marie with foil. Bake for 3 hours, checking from time to time to see if the pan needs more water, or until the flan is set and does not jiggle when moved.

Remove from the bain-marie and allow to cool, then refrigerate overnight.

To unmold, loosen the flan around the edges with a thin metal spatula. Pass the bottom of the loaf pan over a medium flame for about 10 seconds to partly dissolve the caramel, and invert onto a serving platter. Slice and serve with whipped cream.

# Dulce de Leche Panqueque

Dulce de leche is a supersweet caramelized condensed milk. You can make your own of course, but it's quite time-consuming. Because it's nothing more than long-cooked concentrated caramelized milk, this is one of the few store-bought ingredients I find just as delicious as the homemade version.

The first pancake is always tricky, especially if you're using a *chapa* or skillet over a wood fire; you never can be really sure of how hot the cooking surface is until you try it, but the batter makes a generous amount to ensure you have enough for a practice run. This is my kids' favorite dessert. It's mine too. | Serves 6

### FOR THE CREPE BATTER

1½ **cups all-purpose flour**
½ **teaspoon salt**
4 **large eggs**
1 **cup cold water**
1 **cup cold whole milk**
4 **tablespoons unsalted butter, melted**

6 **tablespoons Clarified Butter (page 255)**
6 **heaping tablespoons dulce de leche**

To make the batter, whisk the flour and salt in a medium bowl to combine.

Break the eggs into a large bowl and whisk in the water and milk, then the melted butter. Sift in the flour and salt, whisking to blend. Refrigerate for 1 to 24 hours.

Melt 1 tablespoon of the clarified butter in a crepe pan or cast-iron griddle. When the foam begins to subside, ladle in a generous ¼ cup of batter, tilting the pan to swirl the batter into a thin circle or using a spatula to spread it evenly over the surface. Cook until lightly golden on the bottom, 1 to 2 minutes, then turn and cook the other side for 1 minute. Transfer to a tray and trim the edges, if desired. Repeat with the remaining batter; you want 6 pancakes for this recipe.

Spread each pancake with a heaping tablespoon of dulce de leche, roll up as you would a jelly roll, and serve.

Photographs on pages 232–233

# Tabletón Mendocino

I think of this as the country cousin of the French mille-feuille. It is formed with roughly shaped pastry crackers, layered with dulce de leche (store-bought works fine for this recipe) and dusted with powdered sugar. Make the full recipe even if you're serving fewer people. Somehow it always gets eaten, and any extra crackers taste wonderful just broken into rough pieces. | Serves 12

2 large whole eggs

8 large egg yolks

1 cup dry white wine

8 tablespoons unsalted butter, cut into 1-inch pieces, at room temperature, plus butter for the pans

6 to 7 cups all-purpose flour

3 cups dulce de leche

¼ cup confectioners' sugar

Whisk the eggs and egg yolks together in a large bowl. Whisk in the wine. Transfer ⅓ cup of the egg mixture to a small bowl and work in the butter with your fingers until it forms soft ½-inch clumps. Stir back into the rest of the eggs and gradually work in the flour a cup at a time, using your hands as you would a pastry blender, until the mixture forms a fluffy, somewhat sticky but kneadable mass. Turn it out onto a floured work surface and knead it lightly, adding more flour as necessary until you have a smooth, pliable dough. Divide the dough into 8 pieces. Wrap in plastic wrap and chill for at least 1 hour.

Heat an *horno* or home oven (with the racks positioned in the upper and lower thirds of the oven) to approximately 375°F. Butter four large cookie sheets.

Unwrap one portion of dough; keep the rest of the dough covered until you are ready to roll it out. Roll out the first piece into a rough rectangle about 12 by 16 inches and ⅛ inch thick. Transfer to one half of a cookie sheet, and prick it all over evenly with a fork. Repeat with a second portion of the dough, putting the rolled-out piece on the other half of the first cookie sheet. Repeat with the rest of the dough.

Bake for about 12 minutes, until the *tabletónes* are crisp and resemble large puffy crackers. Cool on racks.

Put one "cracker" on a serving platter and spread with a thin layer of dulce de leche. Cover with a second cracker, and spread with dulce de leche. Repeat until all six layers are stacked and filled (as pictured), or until all eight layers are. (If you wish, save two crackers to break up and serve with an aperitif.) Sprinkle the top with the confectioners' sugar. To slice, use a long serrated knife with a light, sawing motion.

Photograph on page 237

# Breads

I fell in love with the little village of Garzon for its quiet, faded,
but inextinguishable charm.

In every one of my restaurants, from the very first day we opened, we've baked our own bread. It's a daily reaffirmation of who we are, an everyday task that brings its own satisfactions. In a house where bread is baked regularly, it's my experience that you are more likely to find harmony and affection.

Sadly, industrialized baking and farming have deprived us of much of the variety and personality of homemade bread. Bread that is baked to be eaten that day and served as part of the meal has its own unique character. Give two bakers the same ingredients, the same ovens, and the same recipes, and taste the results: they'll always be different. Somehow the bread seems to know who is making it.

# Cremona Bread

Cremona bread, which originated in the Italian town of great violin makers, can be found in Italian bakeries all over Argentina. It's a quick puff pastry made with lard and shaped into a fanciful form. For an even more powerful flavor, try half suet and half lard. | Makes 1 loaf

**1 package active dry yeast**
**About 1¼ cups warm water (100° to 110°F)**
**4 cups all-purpose flour**
**1 tablespoon coarse salt**
**1 tablespoon extra virgin olive oil**
**6 tablespoons melted high-quality lard**

Dissolve the yeast in 1 cup of the warm water. Combine the flour and salt in the bowl of a heavy-duty mixer fitted with the paddle attachment and mix on low speed. Add the olive oil, then gradually add the dissolved yeast. Add up to ¼ cup more warm water as necessary, depending on the flour and humidity, mixing until the dough comes together. Switch to the dough hook and knead on medium speed for about 5 minutes, until the dough is smooth and elastic.

Transfer the dough to the counter, knead it lightly, and shape it into a ball. Place in a large floured bowl, cover with a damp cloth, and let rise in a warm place for about 1 hour, until doubled in size.

Roll the dough out into a rectangle about 8 inches by 24 inches and ¼ inch thick. Trim the edges so they are straight and even. Brush with 2 tablespoons of the melted lard, leaving a ½-inch border all around. Let the dough absorb the lard for about 20 seconds, then fold both short sides into the middle, and fold over in half again. Roll out into a rectangle again and repeat the whole process, to complete two "turns." Let rest, covered, for 30 minutes.

Roll out again into a rectangle about ¼ inch thick and brush with the remaining 2 tablespoons lard. Trim the edges again. Fold the dough over lengthwise again, but leave about ½ inch of the bottom half exposed. With a sharp knife, make even cuts through both layers of dough about ¾ inch apart all along the side with the exposed bottom edge, like a fringe, leaving at least 1 inch uncut along the folded side. Bring the ends of the dough together to form a flat circle with the fringe on the outside.

Put the bread on a floured baking sheet, cover with a damp cloth, and set in a warm place to rise until puffy and light, about 45 minutes.

Heat an *horno* or home oven (with the rack positioned in the lower third of the oven) to approximately 400°F.

Bake for about 30 minutes, until the bread is golden and crisp. Let cool completely on a rack before slicing.

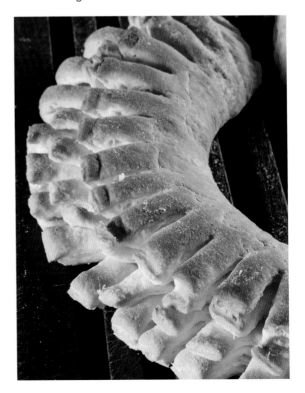

# Pan de Campo

Because of its simplicity and crunchy crust, I think this humble bread is also the most noble. These qualities are symbolic of what bread is supposed to be. It toasts up superbly. If you wrap it carefully in plain brown paper, it can last for weeks in a very dry climate. | Makes 1 large loaf

**1 package active dry yeast**
**1 cup warm water (100° to 110°F)**
**4 to 5 cups all-purpose flour, plus more for dusting**
**1 tablespoon coarse salt**
**1 tablespoon sugar**
**½ cup extra virgin olive oil**

Dissolve the yeast in ½ cup of the warm water.

Combine 4 cups of the flour, the salt, and sugar in the bowl of a heavy-duty mixer fitted with the paddle attachment and mix on low speed. Add the dissolved yeast, olive oil, and remaining ½ cup warm water and mix until combined. Add up to 1 cup more flour as necessary to form a dough that is no longer sticky. Switch to the dough hook and knead for about 8 minutes, until the dough is smooth and elastic.

Transfer the ball of dough into a floured bowl, cover it with a damp towel, and set in a warm place to rise for about 1 hour, until doubled in volume.

Flour a work surface. Punch down the dough. Roll it out into a rough rectangle about 8 inches wide by 15 inches long and ¾ inch thick. Brush the surface lightly with a little water and roll it up lengthwise into a cylinder, evening the sides with your palms. Place on a floured baking sheet, cover with a damp towel, and let rise again for about 1 hour, until almost doubled.

Heat an *horno* or home oven (with the rack positioned in the lower third of the oven) to approximately 350°F.

Cut 4 or 5 diagonal slashes, about ½ inch deep, in the top of the dough. Brush with water and sprinkle with a little flour. Bake for about 45 minutes, until the bread is fragrant, the crust is crisp, and the loaf produces a hollow sound when tapped on the bottom. Cool on a rack.

# Galletas Martin Fierro

To an Argentine, the fictional nineteenth-century gaucho Martin Fierro is the equivalent of the melancholy and righteous character that Clint Eastwood played in his spaghetti westerns. His battles and tribulations rise to the level of mythic heroes, while his everyday life is mean and meager, he is a loner, more at home in the saddle or by the campfire than in town or a comfortable bed on the *estancia*. I created this giant cracker in his honor. It was inspired by a version made in Sevilla called a *regaña*; I thought Fierro would admire its rusticity. It's great with soup or salad. | Makes 4 large crackers; serves 8 to 12

3½ cups all-purpose flour
1 tablespoon active dry yeast
1½ teaspoons coarse salt
1½ teaspoons sugar
1 tablespoon extra virgin olive oil
About 1¼ cups warm water (100° to 110°F)

Combine the flour, yeast, salt, and sugar in the bowl of a heavy-duty mixer fitted with the paddle attachment and mix on low speed. Add the olive oil, then slowly add up to 1¼ cups warm water, mixing until a dough forms. Switch to the dough hook and knead until smooth.

Transfer the dough to a floured bowl, cover with a damp towel, and set in a warm place to rise for about 1 hour, or until about 1½ times its original size—it doesn't need to rise dramatically.

Heat an *horno* or home oven (with the racks positioned in the upper and lower thirds of the oven) to approximately 400°F. Flour two large baking sheets.

Flour a work surface. Punch down the dough and divide it into 4 pieces. Roll out one piece of dough into a rough oval about 8 by 11 inches and as thin as possible—⅛ inch or less. Transfer to a floured baking sheet. Repeat with the remaining dough.

Bake for about 14 minutes, until crisp and lightly browned all over. Cool on a rack. Break into rough pieces to serve.

# Milk Buns

I have always thought that those who forget the dreams of childhood die slowly from the lack of fantasies to sustain our spirits. We can still feel those dreams every day if we take the time. These milk buns, re-created from my childhood memories, never fail to touch the young boy who still lives inside the grown-up. | Makes 6 buns

2 tablespoons unsalted butter
1½ cups whole milk
3 large eggs
About 5 cups all-purpose flour
2 packages active dry yeast
2 tablespoons coarse salt

Heat the butter and milk in a small saucepan over medium-low heat until the butter is melted. Remove from the heat and allow to cool.

Lightly beat 2 of the eggs in a small bowl; set aside.

Combine 4 cups of the flour, the yeast, and salt in the bowl of a heavy-duty mixer with the paddle attachment. With the motor running on low, add the milk and butter to the dry ingredients a little at a time until they are incorporated. Gradually add the beaten eggs, then gradually add up to 1 cup more flour, until a very soft dough forms. Knead for about 10 minutes, until the dough is smooth and elastic.

Transfer the dough to a floured bowl, cover with a damp towel, and set in a warm place to rise for about 1 hour, until doubled in size.

Heat an *horno* or home oven (with the rack positioned in the lower third of the oven) to approximately 350°F.

Turn out the dough onto a floured work surface. Divide it into 6 equal pieces, shape into balls, and gently flatten them with the palms of your hands. Arrange them about 2 inches apart on a large floured baking sheet. Beat the remaining egg in a small bowl and brush the top of each bun with the egg glaze.

Bake for about 20 minutes, until the tops are rounded and glazed a golden brown. Cool on a rack.

# Pan Negro

I prefer this whole-grain bread well toasted, slathered with butter and homemade jam. It's my favorite breakfast. Sliced thin, it's superb for open-faced ham or smoked salmon sandwiches. This is the way the Germans and Swiss would eat their dark bread in Bariloche, the mountain town of my childhood.

| Makes 1 loaf

⅓ cup walnuts

⅓ cup raw almonds

⅓ cup unblanched hazelnuts

2 packages active dry yeast

About 1½ cups warm water (100° to 110°F)

2 cups whole wheat flour

1 cup all-purpose flour, plus more for rolling

½ cup toasted wheat germ

½ cup oat bran

½ cup wheat bran

1 tablespoon coarse salt

2 tablespoons extra virgin olive oil

1 tablespoon honey

Preheat the oven to 300°F.

Scatter the walnuts, almonds, and hazelnuts on a rimmed baking sheet and toast in the oven for about 10 minutes, until fragrant. Remove and allow the nuts to cool on the baking sheet. Coarsely chop the nuts. Set aside.

Dissolve the yeast in 1 cup of the warm water. Combine the flours, wheat germ, oat bran, wheat bran, and salt in the bowl of a heavy-duty mixer fitted with the paddle attachment and mix on low speed. Mix in the dissolved yeast, olive oil, and honey. Gradually add up to ½ cup more warm water, until a dough forms. Switch to the dough hook, add the nuts, and knead for about 10 minutes, until smooth and elastic. Every few minutes, stop the machine and pull the dough apart with your hands to stretch it, then return it to the mixer and continue kneading.

Turn the dough out, shape it into a ball, place it in a floured bowl, and cover with a damp towel. Set in a warm place to rise for about 1 hour, until doubled in size.

Flour a work surface. Flatten the dough with your fingers and roll it out into a rough rectangle about 10 by 18 inches and ¾ inch thick. Brush the surface lightly with a little water and roll it up lengthwise into a cylinder, shaping the sides evenly with your palms.

Place the dough on a floured baking sheet, cover with a damp towel, and let rise again until almost doubled.

Heat an *horno* or home oven (with the rack positioned in the lower third of the oven) to approximately 350°F.

With a sharp knife, cut 4 or 5 slashes about ½ inch deep in the top of the dough. Brush the top with a little water.

Bake for about 45 minutes, until the crust is crisp and the loaf sounds hollow when tapped on the bottom. Allow to cool completely on a rack before slicing.

# Fry Bread

When I was quite young, one of my favorite hiking spots was a mountain called Jakob (named for the Yugoslavian who discovered it). Otto Veiskop, who owned the little farm at the base of this mountain, would always make some fry bread for my friends and me at the end of our walks. Whenever I make skirt steak *a la vara* (page 89), I have a kettle with bubbling lard alongside the fire for fry bread. | Serves 4

**1 package active dry yeast**
**About ⅓ cup warm water (100° to 110°F)**
**2 cups all-purpose flour, plus more for rolling**
**1½ teaspoons salt**
**¼ cup melted high-quality lard**
**Vegetable oil or lard for deep frying**

Dissolve the yeast in ⅓ cup warm water. Combine the flour and salt in the bowl of a heavy-duty mixer fitted with the paddle attachment and mix on low speed. Add the yeast and melted lard and mix until a dough forms; you may need to add a few more tablespoons of water, depending on the flour and the humidity. Switch to the dough hook and knead until the dough is no longer sticky, about 5 minutes.

Turn the dough out and shape it into a ball. Place in a floured bowl, cover with a damp cloth, and let it rise in a warm spot for 45 minutes to 1 hour, until it is doubled in size.

Flour a work surface, turn the dough out, and flatten it with your fingers. Roll it out to a rectangle about 7 by 14 inches and about ¼ inch thick. Cut with a sharp knife into 8 rough squares. Place on a baking sheet, cover with a damp cloth, and let rise for 10 minutes.

Meanwhile, heat the vegetable oil or lard in a *caldero,* deep fryer, or large pot until it sizzles if you dip in a corner of a piece of dough (the temperature should be 375°F). Carefully add 1 or 2 dough squares at a time, and fry, turning, until crisp and golden brown all over, about 3 minutes. Drain on paper towels, and serve hot.

Photograph on page 89

# Chapa Bread

Think Patagonian pita. It's a favorite of campers and hikers. When I was a teenager, I'd make it on camping trips using an inverted cracker tin on top of a *parrilla* for a cooking surface. Now I use a *chapa*. If you're making them on a *chapa* on which you have just cooked meat, cook the bread in the meat drippings.

The dough is the same one called for in Cremona Bread (page 242), but the baking technique is different.

| Makes 8 breads

**4 cups all-purpose flour**
**1 tablespoon coarse salt**
**1 package active dry yeast**
**1 tablespoon extra virgin olive oil**
**About 1¼ cups warm water (100° to 110°F)**

Combine the flour, salt, and yeast in the bowl of a heavy-duty mixer fitted with the paddle attachment and mix on low speed. Add the olive oil, then gradually add the water (more or less, depending on the flour and humidity), until the dough comes together. Switch to the dough hook and knead on medium speed for about 5 minutes, until the dough is smooth and elastic.

Transfer the dough to the counter, knead it lightly, and shape it into a ball. Place in a large floured bowl, cover with a damp cloth, and let rise in a warm place for 45 minutes to 1 hour, until doubled in size.

Roll out the dough to a rectangle about 6 inches by 12 inches and ¼ inch thick (photo 1). Using a sharp knife, cut it into rough 3-inch squares (photo 2). Place on a floured baking sheet, cover with a damp cloth, and let rise in a warm place (near the fire if cooking outdoors on a cold day), until doubled in size, about 30 minutes.

Heat a *chapa* or cast-iron griddle over medium-low heat. Place the breads, in batches, on the *chapa* (photo 3), reduce the heat to low, and cook until puffed and browned on the bottom, about 5 minutes. Flip and brown on the other side (photo 4).

To serve, split open with a knife and fill with your choice of sandwich ingredients.

1

2

3

4

Basics

## Aioli

I first learned to make aioli in Provence, and ever since I have used it on sandwiches, roasts, fish, and simple grilled vegetables. | Makes about 1 cup

**2 large egg yolks, at room temperature**
**3 garlic cloves**
**Coarse salt**
**¾ cup extra virgin olive oil**

Put the egg yolks in a medium bowl. Grate the garlic over the egg yolks with a Microplane (or smash and mince the garlic and add it to the egg yolks). Season with a pinch of salt. Add ¼ cup of the olive oil, a few drops at a time, whisking constantly, until the oil and eggs thicken and emulsify. Whisk in the remaining olive oil in a slow, steady stream, until the aioli is smooth and thick. The aioli can be refrigerated for up to 3 days.

## Black Olive Tapenade

Tapenade can be varied according to whim and what you have on hand. I prefer the tanginess of Kalamata olives to the more subtle Niçoise variety, but either will do. The freshness of the flavors and the texture justify the extra effort of making tapenade from scratch.
| Makes about 1¾ cups

**1 cup pitted Kalamata olives, minced**
**2 tablespoons capers, rinsed, dried, and minced**
**1 teaspoon grated lemon zest**
**1 tablespoon fresh lemon juice**
**1½ teaspoons finely chopped fresh thyme**
**½ cup extra virgin olive oil**
**Freshly ground black pepper**

Combine the olives, capers, lemon zest and juice, and thyme in a medium bowl. Gradually whisk in the olive oil. Season to taste with pepper. The tapenade can be refrigerated for up to 1 week.

## Orange Basil Tapenade

An herbaceous and fruity variation, lovely on tarts or with roast pork. | Makes about 1½ cups

**1 cup pitted Kalamata olives, minced**
**2 tablespoons capers, rinsed, dried, and minced**
**2 teaspoons minced orange zest**
**¼ cup fresh orange juice**
**½ cup packed fresh basil leaves**
**½ cup extra virgin olive oil**

Combine the olives, capers, orange zest, and juice in a medium bowl. Chop the basil very fine and stir it in. Gradually whisk in the olive oil. The tapenade can be refrigerated for up to 1 week.

## Anchovy and Shallot Tapenade

The minced juicy bits of shallots help to marry the briny and strong tastes of anchovies and olives.
| Makes about 1¾ cups

**1 cup pitted Kalamata olives, minced**
**6 anchovy fillets packed in olive oil, rinsed, dried, and minced**
**2 tablespoons capers, rinsed, dried, and finely chopped**
**2 tablespoons finely chopped shallots**
**2 tablespoons minced fresh flat-leaf parsley**
**¼ cup fresh lemon juice**
**½ cup extra virgin olive oil**

Combine the olives, anchovies, capers, shallots, parsley, and lemon juice in a medium bowl. Gradually whisk in the olive oil. The tapenade can be refrigerated for up to 1 week.

## Chimichurri

From gaucho campfires to society weddings, you can always find chimichurri in Argentina. The basics—olive oil, parsley, and oregano—never vary but the rest is up to the ingenuity of the chef and local tradition. Chimichurri changes from town to town. Sometimes I worry that since the world has discovered it, it will get "gourmet-ized" until it's unrecognizable. At a Latin-American-themed James Beard Award evening in New York City, I couldn't believe what some of the chefs had done with it: mango, strawberries, mint! I was so sad, I wanted to crawl inside my oven. Invention is fine, but you have to stay true to the original idea. My variation on the theme is fresh herbs instead of dried, which is what the gauchos use. | Makes about 2 cups

**FOR THE SALMUERA**

**1 cup water**

**1 tablespoon coarse salt**

**1 head garlic, separated into cloves and peeled**

**1 cup packed fresh flat-leaf parsley leaves**

**1 cup fresh oregano leaves**

**2 teaspoons crushed red pepper flakes**

**¼ cup red wine vinegar**

**½ cup extra virgin olive oil**

To make the salmuera, bring the water to a boil in a small saucepan. Add the salt and stir until it dissolves. Remove from the heat and allow to cool.

Mince the garlic very fine and put in a medium bowl. Mince the parsley and oregano and add to the garlic, along with the red pepper flakes. Whisk in the red wine vinegar and then the olive oil. Whisk in the salmuera. Transfer to a jar with a tight-fitting lid, and keep in the refrigerator. Chimichurri is best prepared at least 1 day in advance, so that the flavors have a chance to blend. The chimichurri can be kept refrigerated for up to 2 to 3 weeks.

## Parsley, Olive Oil, and Garlic Sauce

You will find this simple sauce offered in many restaurants as an alternative to chimichurri or salsa criolla.
| Makes about ¾ cup

**½ cup packed minced fresh flat-leaf parsley**

**1 teaspoon minced garlic**

**½ cup extra virgin olive oil**

**Coarse salt and freshly ground black pepper**

Combine the parsley and garlic in a small bowl. Slowly add the olive oil, whisking to combine. The sauce will be bright green and thick with parsley. Season to taste with salt and pepper. The sauce can be kept refrigerated for up to 3 to 4 days.

## Salsa Criolla

*Criollo* refers to Argentines of Spanish or southern European heritage who have developed their own distinct outlook and style. I envision a fellow at the racetrack, a man who dresses meticulously, with a black leather sports coat, a key chain suspended from his belt and a comb tucked into his back pocket, his short hair neatly coiffed with brilliantine.

We use the term *criollo* in cuisine for recipes made with fresh chopped tomato, and often with onion.

Serve with roast chicken, grilled vegetables, and white-fleshed fish. | Makes about 2 cups

**1 large red bell pepper, about 8 ounces**
**1 large red onion, minced**
**¼ cup red wine vinegar**
**Coarse salt and freshly ground black pepper**
**About ½ cup extra virgin olive oil**

Cut the pepper lengthwise in half and remove the stem and seeds. With a very sharp knife, remove all the white pith. Slice into very fine strips, then mince very fine. Transfer to a medium bowl.

Add the minced onion to the peppers and mix well. Stir in the red wine vinegar and season with salt and pepper. Whisk in the olive oil to combine; it should cover the minced onion and pepper. Allow to stand for at least 30 minutes to blend the flavors. The salsa can be refrigerated for up to 3 days.

## Salsa Lucía

This fresh salsa was dreamed up when we were testing our Salt-Crust Chicken (page 132). It's also wonderful with fresh cod, corvina, branzino, and striped bass. It was invented by Lucía Soria, who, while still in her twenties, went from being a cook in my restaurant in Buenos Aires to the manager of Hotel Restaurant Garzon in Uruguay and my second-in-command at important events such as the inaugural dinner for Argentina's president. | Makes about 2 cups

**½ cup pitted Kalamata olives, minced**
**1 tablespoon capers, rinsed, dried, and minced**
**2 tablespoons fresh thyme leaves, minced**
**1 garlic clove, minced**
**1 red bell pepper, minced**
**1 green bell pepper, minced**
**1 small red onion, minced**
**½ teaspoon grated orange zest**
**1 teaspoon crushed red pepper flakes**
**Coarse salt and freshly ground black pepper**
**1 cup extra virgin olive oil**

Combine the olives, capers, thyme, garlic, bell peppers, onion, orange zest, red pepper flakes, and salt and pepper to taste in a medium bowl. Whisk in the olive oil in a slow, steady stream. The salsa can be refrigerated for up to 3 days.

## Sun-Dried Tomatoes

These are quite different from store-bought sun-dried tomatoes. They have intense flavor, but they're not shriveled tomato halves. Instead, they are paper-thin slices, dried flat until they become glazed and translucent. We dry ours in trays on the roof of my hotel in Garzon, but Donna Gelb, who tested all the recipes for this book, made hers on the radiator cover in her apartment in New York City.

If you don't have a Benriner or a meat slicer, you can slice the tomatoes by hand. Choose underripe ones that will slice easily and dry well. | Makes about 2 cups

**4 or 5 slightly underripe large plum tomatoes**
**About 2 cups mild olive oil**

Line several large baking sheets with Silpats, rough side facing up. Slice the tomatoes crosswise paperthin on a Benriner or meat slicer. Lay the slices out in rows on the Silpats. Do not worry about the seeds—they will dry along with the rest of the tomato.

Set the trays out in the sun to dry for a day or so, depending on the weather, or place the trays over or near a radiator. The edges will start to curl up, but when they are completely dry, they will be flat, crisp, and delicate. Carefully lift them one at a time off the pans and layer them in an airtight container or jar. Cover them completely with olive oil. The tomatoes can be refrigerated for at least a week.

## Toasted Fresh Bread Crumbs

Homemade bread crumbs are lighter and have more volume than commercially prepared dried crumbs.
| Makes about 2½ cups

**8 ounces day-old bread, crust removed**
**2 tablespoons extra virgin olive oil**
**Coarse salt and freshly ground black pepper**

Preheat the oven to 375°F.

Crumble the bread into a bowl with your fingers, making small, uneven crumbs. Moisten with the olive oil, and season with salt and pepper.

Turn the crumbs out onto a baking sheet and toast in the oven, tossing occasionally, for 8 to 10 minutes, until golden and crunchy. Let cool. The crumbs can be stored in an airtight container at room temperature for up to 5 days.

## Toasted Almonds

Like all people of Spanish heritage, Argentines consume a lot of almonds. Their blushing pink blossoms are a happy harbinger of the arrival of spring. I like to use them for extra crunch in salads.
| Makes 1 cup

**1 cup sliced almonds**

Preheat the oven to 375°F.

Spread the sliced almonds on a baking sheet. Toast in the oven for about 3 minutes, until they turn golden. Remove from the baking sheet to cool.

## Crispy Garlic Chips

The French have a saying, "You must watch what you're cooking like milk on the stove," referring, of course, to the fact that milk can boil over in a flash. Case in point: Garlic chips are sweet and nutty when cooked just right, but let them go just a little too long, and they become burnt and acrid. | Serves about 4 as a garnish

**4 garlic cloves, as large as possible, peeled**
**1 cup olive oil**

Using a small slicer or a mandoline, slice the garlic very thin.

Heat the olive oil in a 10-inch cast-iron skillet over medium-high heat until very hot. Line a plate with two paper towels. To test the temperature of the oil, add a slice of garlic. If it sizzles, add the rest of the garlic and cook until just crisp and light golden brown, a matter of seconds. Use a flat slotted skimmer to keep the slices from sticking together as they cook, and transfer them to the paper towels to drain the moment they turn color. (The oil can be strained and used for another batch or reserved for another use.)

## Clarified Butter

The flavor that butter adds to a dish is unique and marvelous. Clarifying butter removes the solids that tend to burn and ruin the taste. | Makes about ¾ cup

**½ pound unsalted butter**

Slowly melt the butter in a small heavy saucepan over medium-low heat; do not stir. Remove from the heat, and carefully spoon off all the foam from the top. Pour the clear liquid butter through a fine-mesh strainer lined with cheesecloth, leaving behind the solids in the pan. Once cool, the clarified butter can be refrigerated for weeks.

## Honey Gremolata

Traditional Italian gremolata is sharp, floral, and herbal. I add honey for sweetness, which rounds out the flavor profile. | Makes about 1½ cups

**1 cup fresh flat-leaf parsley leaves, chopped**
**½ cup coarsely chopped fresh oregano**
**1 teaspoon minced garlic**
**¾ teaspoon grated lemon zest**
**1 tablespoon fresh lemon juice**
**1 tablespoon honey**
**1 cup extra virgin olive oil**
**Coarse salt and freshly ground black pepper to**
   **taste**

Whisk all the ingredients together in a bowl. The gremolata can be stored in a tightly sealed jar in the refrigerator for up to 1 week.

# Vinaigrettes and the Language of Ingredients

No written recipe can ever be one hundred percent foolproof. You can't treat a recipe as if it were a manual that tells you how to assemble a lawn mower. The tastes and textures will always vary: the flavors of fruits and vegetables are more concentrated at the peak of the season. Meat tastes different depending on what the animal ate and whether it built up its muscles free-ranging or it spent its whole life in a pen. And then there are the variables of cooking itself: the heat that your fire or stove puts out, the thickness of your pots and pans, the materials from which they're made. A recipe is the start of a three-way conversation between the cook, the ingredients, and the cooking tools.

I received my strongest lesson in this principle when I was in my early twenties and apprenticing at Le Doyen in Paris under Francis Trocellier. The kitchen was a classic brigade, with no less than forty-two chefs and cooks working under the master.

When I arrived, he glanced at my card and said, "So you are a chef?"

At that time, I had my first little restaurant in Bariloche, catering to the après-ski crowd, so my answer to Chef Trocellier's question was yes. But what a difference in scale! If he were the head of the French army and I was in command of the forces of tiny Monaco, you could say we were both generals, but. . . you get the point.

"Well, my young South American, since you're a chef, you'll have lunch with me and my sous-chef every day in the kitchen," Trocellier announced. We were sitting at his table in the kitchen. A waiter poured us each a glass of wine and set a bottle of water in front of us. "I love green salad so all that I ask is that you make me a green salad every day."

"That's all, Chef?" This wasn't a very difficult task. "Surely there's something else I can help with?"

"We'll see. Let's start with that."

The next day, for lunch, I made a green salad and served it to Trocellier. He sniffed, took a mouthful, and tasted as deliberately as a sommelier evaluating a Burgundy.

"I hate it!" he declared. "It's unbalanced." For the next few months, I kept trying, and every day I fell short of the mark. If I couldn't even make a salad dressing, how was I ever going to get to tournedos Rossini or lobster Thermidor?

"You don't know the taste of your ingredients," Trocellier told me one day. "You must listen to your ingredients."

This advice made a big impression.

Finally I got the hang of it. I even threw in some mustard, and he complimented me on that. With that simplest of recipes, I began to learn the language of ingredients. You simply have to taste with an open spirit. You cannot express it in words.

## Red Wine Vinaigrette

To make a great vinaigrette you can't simply pop open a bottle of oil or vinegar you've never used and just follow a written recipe. You have to think through to the end result on the plate and the palate. For example, if you have a mix of delicate greens, you may want the vinegar to be less dominant. Or with a salad of lettuce and poached chicken, you might want to increase the amount of vinegar or use sharper vinegar.

Years ago, when making chimichurri, I started to use salmuera, salt dissolved in water, rather than simply seasoning it with dry salt. I like the way the saltiness diffuses and rounds out the other flavors. I now do this with my vinaigrettes as well. | Makes about ½ cup

**2 tablespoons red wine vinegar**
**½ teaspoon coarse salt, dissolved in 1 teaspoon boiling water**
**⅛ teaspoon freshly ground black pepper**
**5 tablespoons extra virgin olive oil**

Combine the vinegar, salmuera (salted water), and pepper in a small bowl. Whisk in the olive oil in a slow, steady stream. The vinaigrette can be refrigerated for up to 3 days.

## Lemon Vinaigrette

Makes about ½ cup

**2 tablespoons fresh lemon juice**
**½ teaspoon coarse salt, dissolved in 1 teaspoon boiling water**
**⅛ teaspoon freshly ground black pepper**
**6 tablespoons extra virgin olive oil**

Combine the lemon juice, salmuera (salted water), and pepper in a small bowl. Whisk in the olive oil in a slow, steady stream. The vinaigrette can be refrigerated for up to 3 days.

## Mustard Vinaigrette

Makes about ½ cup

**1 tablespoon Dijon mustard**
**1 tablespoon red wine vinegar**
**½ teaspoon coarse salt, dissolved in 1 teaspoon boiling water**
**Freshly ground black pepper**
**¼ cup extra virgin olive oil**

Combine the mustard, vinegar, salmuera (salted water), and pepper to taste in a small bowl. Whisk in the olive oil in a slow, steady stream. If the vinaigrette seems too thick, whisk in a tablespoon of water. The vinaigrette can be refrigerated for up to 3 days.

## Lemon Confit

The combination of fruitiness, bitterness, and a floral bouquet in a lemon confit helps to focus and refine the powerful flavor of grilled meat, poultry, and fish.

| Makes about 2½ cups

**4 lemons**
**2 bay leaves**
**8 black peppercorns**
**About 2 cups extra virgin olive oil**
**½ cup dry white wine**
**1 teaspoon coarse salt**

Cut the lemons in half. Squeeze the juice and reserve it for another use.

Put the squeezed lemon halves in a large saucepan and add the bay leaves, peppercorns, 2 tablespoons of the olive oil, the white wine, and salt. Add enough water to completely cover the lemons and bring to a boil. Reduce the heat and cook gently over medium-low heat until the lemon peel is tender, about 25 minutes. Remove from the heat and allow to cool in the liquid.

Drain the lemons and tear the peel into rough strips about 1 inch wide. Place a strip of lemon peel skin side down on the work surface and, using a sharp paring knife, scrape away every bit of the white pith, leaving only the yellow zest. Repeat with the remaining peel.

Put the strips of lemon zest in a small container and cover completely with olive oil. The confit will keep tightly covered in the refrigerator, for at least a week.

## Orange Confit

Makes about 3 cups

**4 oranges**
**3 bay leaves**
**12 black peppercorns**
**About 2¼ cups extra virgin olive oil**
**¾ cup dry white wine**
**2 teaspoons coarse salt**

Cut the oranges in half. Squeeze the juice and reserve it for another use.

Put the squeezed orange halves in a large saucepan and add the bay leaves, peppercorns, 3 tablespoons of the olive oil, the white wine, and salt. Add enough water to completely cover the oranges and bring to a boil. Reduce the heat and cook until the orange peel is tender, about 25 minutes. Remove from the heat and allow to cool in the liquid.

Drain the oranges and tear the peel into rough strips about 1 inch wide. Place a strip of orange peel skin side down on the work surface and, using a very sharp paring knife, scrape away every bit of the white pith, leaving only the orange zest. Repeat with the remaining peel.

Put the strips of orange zest in a small container and cover completely with olive oil. The confit will keep tightly covered in the refrigerator, for at least a week.

## Charred Sweet Potato Strips

You can serve these instead of French fries with anything from grilled steak to roasted fish or chicken. They are a nice balance of charred, crisp, savory, and slightly sweet. They also add attractive color. | Serves 4

**3 sweet potatoes, scrubbed**
**¼ cup extra virgin olive oil**
**Coarse salt**

Using a mandoline or Benriner, slice the potatoes lengthwise into ⅛-inch-thick strips. Toss with the olive oil.

Heat a *chapa* or large cast-iron griddle over medium-high heat until a drop of water sizzles on the surface. Working in batches, lay out the sweet potatoes in an uncrowded layer on the hot surface and cook, without moving them, for about 4 minutes, until nicely charred on the bottom. Turn and cook for about 2 more minutes, until tender. Serve immediately, sprinkled with coarse salt.

## Rescoldo Bell Peppers and Onions

I love this divine combination alongside meat, fish, or poultry. Like all *rescoldo* recipes, it is so easy and requires very little bother while you attend to your fire and main courses. | Serves 4 to 6

**4 red bell peppers**
**4 medium white onions, unpeeled**
**Coarse salt and freshly ground black pepper**
**Extra virgin olive oil**

Prepare a bed of embers (see page 22).

Bury the whole peppers and onions in the embers, making sure they are completely and evenly covered. Let them roast for 10 minutes. Spread the embers apart and, using tongs, turn the vegetables. Replace the embers and cook for another 10 minutes, adjusting the coals and embers as necessary for even cooking.

Carefully dig out the peppers and onions, taking care not to break them. Clean off the ashes with a cloth or paper towels. Remove the outside layers of the onions. Peel the peppers, then core them and remove the seeds and membranes. Tear the peppers into 2-inch-wide strips. Split the onions in half. Season to taste with salt and pepper and drizzle with a little olive oil.

## Roasted Peppers

When I don't have access to wood fire and embers for the *rescoldo* method, here is how I make roasted peppers indoors. | Serves 4

**4 red bell peppers**
**About ¼ cup extra virgin olive oil**

Preheat the broiler. Line a broiler pan with aluminum foil and put the peppers on it. Place the peppers under the broiler, close to the heat, and allow them to blister and char, turning occasionally to expose all sides to the heat, until the peppers are blackened on all sides.

Remove from the broiler, cover the peppers with another sheet of foil, and seal the edges tightly so they will steam. Let stand for 10 minutes, then open the foil and allow the peppers to cool.

Remove the cores and seeds from the peppers and discard. With a small sharp knife, scrape away the charred skin; wipe away any remaining bits of skin or seeds with a paper towel. Put the peppers in a dish and cover with the olive oil. They can be refrigerated for up to 3 days.

## Rescoldo Eggplants

Soft, smoky eggplant is just about the perfect partner for hearty roast meats. | Serves 4

**2 medium eggplants**
  **(choose eggplants of the same size)**

Prepare the embers (see page 22).

Bury the eggplants in the embers, making sure they are completely and evenly covered. Roast for 10 minutes. Part the embers and check the eggplants for tenderness by piercing them with a bamboo skewer. If you will be grilling them later don't let them get too soft. If they need a few more minutes in the embers, use tongs to turn them, then replace the embers and cook for another 5 minutes or so, adjusting the coals and embers as necessary for even cooking. Carefully dig out the eggplants, and wipe off the ashes with a cloth or paper towels. Cut the eggplants lengthwise in half. Arrange on a platter and serve.

When it comes time to sit down to eat, it doesn't matter to me how people dress or speak, how they look or sound or even smell. They're all beautiful if they share one simple quality: respect for the meal, the moment, and one another—those who cook, those who serve, and those who eat.

Such people are always welcome at my table.

# Sources

**12-INCH ROUND SKILLET**

### Cast-Iron Skillets, Griddles, Dutch Ovens, and Camp Ovens

Lodge preseasoned cast iron is the best substitute for a *chapa*. Recipes in this book calling for a *chapa* can also be cooked on 10- or 12-inch round skillets or on griddles; a 12-inch square griddle, which has a larger surface area than the 12-inch round; or the two-burner Pro-Grid Reversible Griddle.

For *caldero* recipes, use a 5- or 7-quart Dutch oven. For an iron box, use either size Dutch oven or a 5-quart lidded chicken fryer. Footed camp Dutch ovens can be placed directly over coals. www.lodgemfg.com

**PRO-GRID REVERSIBLE GRIDDLE**

### Fireplace Tools and Fireproof Gloves

Long-handled iron tongs for moving wood around, a big-headed spatula, a charcoal and ash hoe, extra-long suede gloves, and a Tuscan grill are available at Steven Raichlen's store. You can use a standard fireplace grate for an improvised fire basket to let coals drop through. www.barbecuebible.com

### Adjustable Fireplace Grill

The Spitjack Fireplace Grill has a 3-level adjustable grate and a built-in drip pan to help prevent flare-ups. www.spitjack.com

### Wood-Fired Ovens and Hornos

These are now widely available. A variety of styles for indoor or outdoor use are imported from Sardinia by Los Angeles Ovenworks. www.losangelesovenworks.com

**5-QUART DUTCH OVEN**

### Fire Rings

A wide selection of five rings can be found online at www.onlinesports.com

**CHARCOAL AND ASH HOE**

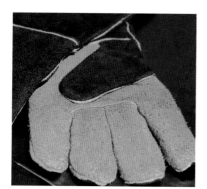

FIREPROOF GLOVES

### Kitchen Tongs

Oxo makes strong 12-inch nylon-headed tongs that don't pierce your meat or scratch your pans. They also make 18-inch long-handled barbecue tongs with wide tips for turning vegetables while cooking in ashes and embers, as well as an easy-to-read oven thermometer and a 13-inch splatter screen. www.oxo.com

### Meat Pounder

Bridge Kitchenware has a selection of heavyweight professional-quality stainless-steel meat pounders. The round model is compact and comes in a variety of weights. www.bridgekitchenware.com

### Thermometers and Spatulas

For salt-crust recipes, simple thermometers that can be left in meat or fish while baking are available at most supermarkets.

Sophisticated digital styles with an instant-read metal probe on a long stainless-steel wire and an alarm that goes off when the desired temperature is reached can be used for checking internal temperature of smaller cuts of meat and steaks on the grill, as well as roasts and home-oven salt crusting.

A laser thermometer is useful for checking oven temperatures in different areas of an *horno.* A large frying thermometer is also very helpful.

A 4-inch wood-handled stainless-steel scraper is almost identical to the putty knife used in some recipes. That and a solid offset spatula are useful for delicate flipping and transferring. www.cooking.com

SPITJACK FIREPLACE GRILL

A WOOD-FIRED HORNO

12-INCH NYLON-HEADED TONGS

# Acknowledgments

This book is the result of many years, many experiences, many friendships, many mentors, and many hours spent in front of a fire. I would like to thank all the members of my professional family in Buenos Aires, Mendoza, and Uruguay and, of course, the generations of Mallmanns who have taught me, tasted with me, and supported me with love and a healthy appetite.

I am immensely grateful to the quartet of people pictured on this page: Lucía Soria, who is my dear friend and a wonderful chef; Donna Gelb, who explored the world of wood-fire cookery and made it accessible to the North American kitchen; Vanina Chimeno, whose spirit and whose cooking has been part of my life for the last eleven years; and Santiago Soto Monllor, who worked so creatively and diligently as the main photographer for this book. My agent, Lisa Queen, made this book possible by bringing it to the immensely warm and perceptive Ann Bramson, publisher of Artisan. Ann and her team at Artisan are chiefly responsible for bringing my chef's vision to the printed page: I appreciate Judith Sutton's copy editing, Jan Derevjanik's design and art direction, Erin Sainz's support, Nancy Murray's careful supervision of the printing; and Trent Duffy's indefatigable dedication to getting every word right. And this book simply wouldn't have been possible without my friend and colleague, Peter Kaminsky; by now, I think of him and his whole family as part of my own family.

Thanks are also due to Sebastian Hernandez, Jose Cabral, Orlando Diaz Masa, Fabian Muñoz, Hugo Ojeda, Nicolas Cordeiro, Fernando Hara, Sebastián Bertalmio, Adrian Perez Plada, Mariano Guiu, Luis Garcia, Javier Luengo, Ambar Rosa Mallmann, Allegra Mallmann, Alexia Mallmann, Francisco Mallmann, Andino Mallmann, Carlos Mallmann, Picho Mallmann, Mark Kelly, Marie Ducate, and Grace Kwon.

Lucía Soria, chef

Donna Gelb, recipe chef

Vanina Chimeno, chef

Santiago Soto Monllor, principal photographer

# Index

## Photo Credits

**Santiago Solo Monllor:** pages ii–iii, vi, x, 8 (left), 10, 13, 15, 16, 19, 20, 23 (both), 24, 27, 30, 33, 39, 41 (both), 42, 44–45 (both), 48–49 (both), 50 (all), 53, 57 (all), 58, 59, 62, 63, 64, 66, 68, 76 (right), 77 (all), 80 (both), 83 (both), 85, 86 (both), 87, 88, 89, 91 (both), 93, 95 (both), 96 (all), 100–101, 102, 103, 105 (both), 106–7 (all), 108, 115, 119, 124 (both), 125, 127 (both), 128, 129, 130–31 (all), 133, 134, 136, 140, 144–45 (both), 157 (all), 158, 163, 167, 168, 171 (all), 172, 173, 174, 175 (all), 178, 179, 180, 183, 184, 187, 188, 189, 192–93 (both), 197, 198, 205, 209, 212, 213, 216, 217, 221, 222–23, 224 (both), 227, 228, 229, 231, 232 (both), 233, 237, 238, 240, 241, 242, 247, 249 (all), 256 (both), 263, and 268 (all).

**The Companion Group:** pages 264 (bottom) and 265 (top).

**Virginia Del Giudice:** pages viii, 2, 6, 120–21 (both), 149, and 202–3 (both).

**Miki Duisterhof:** pages 52, 72, 110, 148, 162, and 250.

**Peter Kaminsky:** pages 9 (left), 71, 147, and 155.

**Lodge Cast Iron Cookware:** page 264 (top three).

**Los Angeles Ovenworks:** page 265 (second from bottom).

**Jason Lowe:** pages 9 (right), 29, 73, 75, 78–79, 99, 111, 152–53 (all), 169, 218, and 236.

**Francis Mallmann:** pages v, 8 (right), 32, 38, 76 (left), 92, 113, 122, 135, 139, 156, 181, 207, 208, and 264.

**Oxo:** page 265 (bottom).

**SpitJack:** page 265 (second from top).

**Pablo Stubrin:** page 201 (both).

Map on page 1 by James Williamson.

## Restaurants (and Hotel) of Francis Mallmann

**Patagonia Sur**
Rocha 801 (corner of Pedro de Mendoza)
La Boca
Buenos Aires, Argentina
Telephone*: +54-11-4303-5917
www.restaurantepatagoniasur.com

**Hotel & Restaurant Garzon**
Garzon, Uruguay
Telephone*: +598-410-2811
www.restaurantgarzon.com

**Francis Mallmann 1884**
Belgrano 1188
Godoy Cruz
Mendoza, Argentina
Telephone*: +54-261-424-2698
www.1884restaurante.com.ar

*Dial your international access code
(011 in the United States) first.

# Conversion Tables

Here are rounded-off equivalents between the metric system and the traditional systems that are used in the United States to measure weight and volume.

## WEIGHTS

| US/UK | Metric |
|---|---|
| ¼ oz | 7 g |
| ½ oz | 15 g |
| 1 oz | 30 g |
| 2 oz | 55 g |
| 3 oz | 85 g |
| 4 oz | 110 g |
| 5 oz | 140 g |
| 6 oz | 170 g |
| 7 oz | 200 g |
| 8 oz (½ lb) | 225 g |
| 9 oz | 250 g |
| 10 oz | 280 g |
| 11 oz | 310 g |
| 12 oz | 340 g |
| 13 oz | 370 g |
| 14 oz | 400 g |
| 15 oz | 425 g |
| 16 oz (1 lb) | 450 g |

## VOLUME

| American | Imperial | Metric |
|---|---|---|
| ¼ tsp | | 1.25 ml |
| ½ tsp | | 2.5 ml |
| 1 tsp | | 5 ml |
| ½ Tbsp (1½ tsp) | | 7.5 ml |
| 1 Tbsp (3 tsp) | | 15 ml |
| ¼ cup (4 Tbsp) | 2 fl oz | 60 ml |
| ⅓ cup (5 Tbsp) | 2½ fl oz | 75 ml |
| ½ cup (8 Tbsp) | 4 fl oz | 125 ml |
| ⅔ cup (10 Tbsp) | 5 fl oz | 150 ml |
| ¾ cup (12 Tbsp) | 6 fl oz | 175 ml |
| 1 cup (16 Tbsp) | 8 fl oz | 250 ml |
| 1¼ cups | 10 fl oz | 300 ml |
| 1½ cups | 12 fl oz | 350 ml |
| 1 pint (2 cups) | 16 fl oz | 500 ml |
| 2½ cups | 20 fl oz (1 pint) | 625 ml |
| 5 cups | 40 fl oz (1 qt) | 1.25 l |

## OVEN TEMPERATURES

| | °F | °C | Gas Mark |
|---|---|---|---|
| very cool | 250–275 | 130–140 | ½–1 |
| cool | 300 | 148 | 2 |
| warm | 325 | 163 | 3 |
| moderate | 350 | 177 | 4 |
| moderately hot | 375–400 | 190–204 | 5–6 |
| hot | 425 | 218 | 7 |
| very hot | 450–475 | 232–245 | 8–9 |